MARTHA · STEWART'S
CHRISTMAS

The snow turned all to pearl, the dark trees strung with pearls,
the sky beginning to flow with such a radiance as never was on
land or sea. And the stillness everywhere . . .

Gladys Hasty Carroll

MARTHA·STEWART'S
CHRISTMAS

PHOTOGRAPHY
CHRISTOPHER BAKER

DESIGN
VIRGINIA EDWARDS

CLARKSON N. POTTER, INC./PUBLISHERS, NEW YORK

To all members of my family
and to all my friends
who are always there when I need them,
love and peace.
And,
joy to the world.

PUBLISHED BY CLARKSON N. POTTER, INC., 201 EAST 50TH STREET, NEW YORK, NEW YORK 10022, AND DISTRIBUTED BY CROWN PUBLISHERS, INC.
CLARKSON N. POTTER, POTTER, AND COLOPHON ARE TRADEMARKS OF CLARKSON N. POTTER, INC.

MANUFACTURED IN JAPAN

LIBRARY OF CONGRESS CATALOGING-IN-PUBLICATION DATA
STEWART, MARTHA.
[CHRISTMAS]
MARTHA STEWART'S CHRISTMAS: ENTERTAINING, DECORATING & GIVING/BY MARTHA STEWART.

P. CM.
1. CHRISTMAS DECORATIONS. 2. CHRISTMAS COOKERY. 3. ENTERTAINING.
I. TITLE. II. TITLE: CHRISTMAS.
TT900.C4S733 1989 793.2'2—DC20 89-8672

ISBN 0-517-57416-0
1 3 5 7 9 10 8 6 4 2
FIRST EDITION

ACKNOWLEDGMENTS

This, of all my books, was the most spontaneous. My publisher and I were chatting one September afternoon about our holiday plans, and Alan, who had been to my Christmas parties in previous years, said, "Would you like to do a book on Christmas entertaining?"

I loved the idea, and suggested that for this book to have the warmth and friendliness of our family Christmas, we should write and photograph it in real time, starting right after Thanksgiving, and ending on Christmas Day. And that's what we did, recording recipes as we made gifts and meals for our family and friends, scribbling in notebooks while the children decorated the Christmas tree, and inviting the photographer to our annual all-over-the-house buffet.

Because this book is about our very own Christmas, it involved my dearest friends and family. My sister Laura Herbert loved this project and gave it much of her time. My mother, Martha Kostyra, baked and gave us lots of her favorite recipes. Rita Christiansen kept my office running smoothly and also baked and donated wonderful Norwegian recipes. My brother George Christiansen offered moral support (and construction advice). My daughter, Alexis, helped decorate the house in her inimitable fashion, working quietly and quickly.

My friend Melissa Neufeld sent props, dishes, and ideas from her home in California, and came to help for the week before the party. Zacki Murphy spent almost five weeks in Connecticut creating, cooking, and decorating. Lisa Wagner was my New York liaison, shopping early in the mornings for the ingredients we could not find in Westport. Julia Pemberton and Maria Calise cooked and cooked. Sal Gilbertie contributed wonderful herbs to our kitchen; Katy van Acker supplied much good humor. Necy Fernandes and Dirce Martins ran the house; Renato and Renaldo Abreu hung wreaths, set up trees, and wired little white lights everywhere. Larry Kennedy drove back and forth to New York gathering props and foodstuffs. Winston Powell brought a wonderful staff to my party to wait and tend bar.

Christopher Baker took all the photographs, calmly and beautifully. This is the third book we have done together, and I so appreciate his fine talent. Virginia Edwards, with initial support from Coleman Souter of San Francisco, spent many hours designing and redesigning this book to squeeze in all the material and somehow still make it clear and beautiful.

At Clarkson N. Potter, the staff was indefatigable: Alan Mirken, having sparked the book, watched over its progress; Gael Towey supervised the design through the last days of her pregnancy; Carol Southern offered helpful editorial advice; Laurie Stark, Ed Otto, Teresa Nicholas, and Amy Schuler took care of myriad production details. My editor, Isolde Motley, did a fantastic job coordinating everyone and everything; she was always encouraging, and always enthusiastic.

My special thanks go to the Greens Farms Academy carolers, whose beautiful voices gave so much to our party; and to my littlest friends: Peter Beer, Christen Hartnett, Sophie Martha Herbert, Wendy Noël, Monica Pasternak, Olivia and Katharine Zaleski, and their parents.

TABLE OF CONTENTS

It seems like yesterday, that early Christmas morning when I crept down the chilly oak staircase in our family home in Nutley to steal a glance at the beautifully decorated tree and the piles of presents beneath it. Even then, I was the first to wake in our crowded household; after the weeks of preparation, the baking and decorating and present making with my younger brothers and sisters, I just couldn't wait for dawn.

Then, as now, I loved the *idea* of Christmas. I loved the story of the Savior's birth, the music of Bach and Handel, the carols we sang at school, the big crêche in front of our church, the strings of lights crisscrossing Franklin Avenue, the electric candles in our neighbors' windows.

My mother used to start her Christmas prep-arations in the summer, and so do I, picking berries for jams and jellies, drying the herbs and flowers that will go into our potpourri and deco-rations. But the season really begins on the day after Thanksgiving, when I make my plum pud-dings. The last week of November is spent mak-ing more conserves and condiments, and taking our

Opposite: Three 19th-century glass pedestals, tiered like a pyramid, hold sugared fruit—"sugarplums."

Above: At Christmas, the house glows with warmth and light, and wonderful scents waft around doors.

summer stock from the pantry to be prettily packaged. When December begins, the house fills with scent as the children mix potpourri in our deep kitchen sinks. Then there's our cookie marathon, when the entire family is drafted to mix, roll, cut out, and decorate the confections that will be packed up as gifts, or served up for parties.

Once the gift baskets have been filled and sent on their way, it's time to deck the halls: the children are turned into foragers, searching for pinecones and seed pods that will be gilded and sparkled into extraordinary decorations. Choosing the Christmas tree is a great ceremony, and then there's the fun of making ornaments—the children made hundreds of popcorn balls this year.

The second week of December is set aside for party preparation: making the great cassoulet, the biscuits and rolls, baking the hams. Then it's truly Christmas, time for opening gifts, breakfast with the family, a quiet dinner with friends, candlelight and carols, time to remember Christmases past. This is, to me, the most joyous of holidays, and I've gathered together here all my favorite memories and ideas to help make this season as meaningful for others as it has been for me and my family.

During the first snowfall in December, I decorated the outside of the house for the Christmas party. The pillars were wrapped with roping of white pine, fir wreaths were hung on every window, and tiny white lights were strung in the apple trees outside.

. . . the raisins were so plentiful and rare, the almonds so extremely
white, the other spices so delicious, the candied fruits so caked and
spotted with molten sugar as to make the coldest lookers-on feel faint .
Charles Dickens

Family traditions evolve over time, and one of my favorites is the yearly creation of the plum pudding. I made my very first shortly after my marriage, on the day after Thanksgiving. A friend and I concocted the recipe from old English cookbooks, and I served the pudding to our friends that Christmas, doused with brandy and mounds of creamy hard sauce. Word spread and requests poured in for puddings for next year. To keep up with the demand, I began collecting traditional English pudding bowls [in brown and white glazed pottery]; I invented an oven-cooking method so we could cook thirty-two puddings every six hours; I discovered that the fruit could be chopped in a food processor a little at a time. This Christmas, with just one helper, we made three hundred puddings in less than three days. While you may not wish to produce puddings on quite such a grand scale, this is one of the most wonderful gifts you can give—at least to your ten dearest friends.

Opposite: Dozens of bowls hold the
ingredients for 100 plum puddings—
ten times the recipe—which we made
in one giant batch.

Above: A garden urn drifted with
snow beside the frozen swimming pool.

MARTHA STEWART'S CHRISTMAS PUDDING

MAKES 10, EACH SERVING 10 TO 15

- 5 pounds dried currants
- 6 cups cognac or brandy
- 30 thin slices white bread
- 6 cups apple cider
- 5 pounds dark raisins, finely chopped
- 2½ pounds candied orange peel, finely chopped
- 2½ pounds candied lemon peel, finely chopped
- 2½ pounds candied citron, finely chopped
- 5 pounds shelled walnuts, finely chopped
- 10 cups all-purpose flour
- 10 teaspoons baking soda
- 10 teaspoons salt
- 10 teaspoons ground cinnamon
- 2½ teaspoons grated nutmeg
- 7½ teaspoons ground mace
- 4 pounds fresh ground suet
- 10 cups packed dark brown sugar
- 30 large eggs, beaten
- 3 cups black currant jam or preserves

Soak the currants in 1 cup of cognac and enough apple cider to cover until plumped, at least 30 minutes. Soak bread slices in remaining apple cider. Oil 10 2-quart pudding molds or pottery bowls with vegetable oil. Preheat the oven to 300° F.

Combine the plumped currants with the remaining fruits and walnuts in a large bowl. Sift together the flour, baking soda, salt, and spices and add to the fruit and nut mixture. Add the suet, bread, apple cider, brown sugar, eggs, and jam and blend well. Beat with a wooden spoon to lighten the mixture.

Spoon the mixture into the molds and cover tightly with rounds of moistened parchment paper secured by rubber bands. Place molds in large roasting pans, and then fill pans with boiling water. Cover molds and pan with aluminum foil and steam in the oven for 5 to 6 hours, adding boiling water as necessary.

Remove the molds from the pans and uncover the puddings. Pour ½ cup of cognac or brandy over each one and re-cover with a circle of wax paper and a fresh piece of moistened parchment paper. Set molds in a cool place (a low shelf of the refrigerator) to ripen.

To serve an individual pudding, steam on a rack in a large pot for 2 more hours. Loosen sides of pudding with a thin metal spatula and invert the mold carefully onto a serving platter. Mix a teaspoon of sugar and a ½ cup of cognac, heat, pour over the warm pudding, and flame with a match. Serve with Hard Sauce or Brandy Sauce (both page 16).

Opposite above: I worked in the sunny end of the kitchen at a table on which I placed bowls holding the ingredients for the puddings.

Opposite below: Batter jugs holding the cider and the cognac were ranked along the windowsill.

Above: The mixture was so heavy I thought the wooden spoon would break and used my hands instead to blend and break up any lumps.

HARD SAUCE

MAKES 2 CUPS

1 *cup (2 sticks) unsalted butter*
2 *cups sifted confectioners' sugar*
1 *large egg yolk*
4 *tablespoons heavy cream*
4 *tablespoons cognac*

Whip the butter and confectioners' sugar together until smooth and creamy. Beat in the egg yolk, cream, and cognac.

BRANDY SAUCE

MAKES 1 CUP

½ *cup heavy cream*
4 *tablespoons (½ stick) unsalted butter, at room temperature*
½ *cup sugar*
2 *large egg yolks, lightly beaten*
2 *tablespoons cognac*

In a small heavy saucepan, bring the cream to a boil. Stir in the butter and sugar. Pour some of this mixture into the egg yolks, whisking to prevent curdling. Return egg-yolk mixture to the pan and simmer, stirring constantly, just until the mixture thickens; do not boil. Remove from heat and stir in cognac.

The steamed puddings in a mélange of pottery bowls, topped with fresh parchment. I found that wetting the parchment helps it mold well to the shape of the bowl, and a rubber band assures a tight covering.

POMANDERS & POTPOURRI

Lo, how a rose e'er blooming, from tender root has sprung
To all the world bestowing, what men of old have sung.
Michael Praetorius

When I first moved to Westport, I attended a garden-club lecture about potpourris. I was just beginning my flower gardens, and I was very interested to learn how to preserve not only the beauty of the flowers, but also their scents. Fifteen years later, many of us are aware of the pleasure in gently scenting our homes with natural perfumes. Wonderfully aromatic—and decorative—potpourris and pomanders are available from florists and perfumers, but they are also really simple to make. If you are a gardener, dry as many flowers, herbs, and seed pods as you can during the summer and fall, then gather them together just before Christmas to make a potpourri with your own garden scent. Weekend foraging trips can provide all sorts of woodland treasures to make pomanders, nut balls, and nut trees. My nephew Christopher and niece Sophie were especially helpful in creating the gifts and decorations you'll find on the next few pages.

Opposite: The green Household enamel cookstove in the old kitchen was the perfect place to display our fragrant potpourri and spicy pomander balls.

Above: One rose escaped my potpourri and was dried by the winter cold.

POMANDERS, NUT TREES, AND SPICE BALLS

Filberts
Chestnuts
Walnuts
Almonds
Brazil nuts
Pecans
Whole nutmegs
Whole cloves
Allspice berries
Juniper berries
Dried rosehips
Miniature pinecones
Sheet mosses

1. A plastic foam sphere was used as the base for this decorative nut ball. Each filbert is affixed with a dab of hot wax from the "glue" gun.

2. Tiny pinecones from Laura's hemlock trees are inserted carefully between the filberts: it is important to cover the entire surface of the plastic foam—there should be no glimpses of white.

NOTE: *Hot-glue guns are available in most hobby and hardware stores and crafts departments.*

Opposite above: The basic ingredients for the creation of nut trees, balls, and other decorative objects together with the foam shapes and, of course, a good hot-glue gun with lots of wax sticks.

Opposite below: A sampling of the unusual and appealing nut and spice balls, which will make delightful gifts and decorations, atop a fabulous 19th-century Amish silk coverlet.

OUR GARDEN
POTPOURRI

Bay leaves
Allspice berries
Bayberry bark
Eucalyptus leaves
Whole cloves
Whole star anise
Juniper berries
Lavender
Rosehips
Giant whole nutmegs
Dried orange and lemon peel
Tellicherry peppercorns
Cinnamon sticks
Orrisroot powder
Senna pods
Lemongrass
Hibiscus
Chamomile
Rose petals and buds
Poppy seed pods
Globe amaranth
Lemon verbena leaves
Blue malva
Marigolds
Cornflowers
Flower oils: lavender, tea rose,
rose geranium

*Above: Five-year-old Monica
Pasternak helped mix my potpourri
this year.*

*Left: A walnut burl bowl crafted by
my older brother Eric is filled with a
very special potpourri.*

*Opposite: Teeny and Weeny, our new
blue point Himalayan kittens, survey
the porch table laden with bowls and
baskets of potpourri ingredients.*

*Following pages: The basic, lightly
oil-scented potpourri mixture is spooned
into cellophane florists' bags. The
whole dried rose blossoms and poppy
seed pods are carefully placed on top.*

CONSERVES & CONDIMENTS

Let the bright red berries glow,
Everywhere in goodly show.
German carol

I was brought up in the aftermath of World War II, amid large victory gardens and a "save for the morrow" mentality. On summer visits to my grandmother Ruszkowski I picked cherries, strawberries, grapes, and peaches and learned about preserving. She had a fabulous collection of old jars and lids which were used over and over again as, every year, she gave masses of gifts from her larder—with the proviso that each and every jar be returned, with its lid.

I still do lots of preserving for Christmas giving, and so do my friends. Salli LaGrone picks berries in the Tennessee mountains for her jams; Helen Brandt concocts wonderful jellies; Inez Norwich pickles her quail eggs; and my sister Kathy makes flavored oils and vinegars. The se-

cret, for all of us, is to be organized so that when the berries are ripe or the tomatoes juicy, the jars and lids are clean and the paraffin ready for melting. Then, when Christmas draws near, we have shelves upon shelves of jars, colorful as jewels, ready for giving.

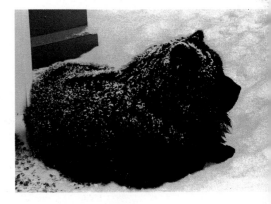

Opposite: I search garage sales for the old green- and blue-glass lidded jars with the metal clamps or lead tops, and am always on the lookout for old-fashioned clear-glass jelly jars.

Above: My chow chow, Blue Max. Dusted with snow, he looks like something out of the pages of Dr. Zhivago.

RED HOT PRESERVES

MAKES 4 PINTS

6½ cups sugar
1½ cups cider vinegar
1 cup finely diced orange bell pepper
1 cup finely diced red bell pepper
1 cup finely diced yellow bell pepper
½ cup finely diced chile pepper
½ teaspoon salt
3 ounces liquid fruit pectin
Sprigs fresh rosemary

In a heavy saucepan, bring sugar, vinegar, peppers, and salt to a boil. Lower the heat and simmer for 10 minutes. Bring to a boil again, add pectin, and boil for 1 minute, stirring constantly. Remove from heat and skim.

Pour preserves into hot, sterilized jars, add a rosemary sprig to each, and seal.

HOT PEPPER VODKA

MAKES 1 PINT

2 long hot red peppers
2 long hot green peppers
1 pint good vodka

Add the peppers to the container of vodka and refrigerate or freeze for at least 1 week.

Opposite: Many stores sell the clamp-topped French-style canning jars. They are more expensive than Ball or Kerr jars, but are totally reusable, and very attractive. Pretty clamp-top bottles, plain or with molded decorations, look beautiful with a bit of ribbon round the neck—or unadorned, with their flavored vodka or scented vinegar contents. (In my own kitchen, I use a big green bottle fitted with a bar-pouring spout to hold dish liquid.)

LEMON VODKA

MAKES 1 QUART

4 lemons
1 quart good vodka

Using a citrus stripper, remove lemon rinds in long, thin strips. Add the lemon rind to the container of vodka and place in the freezer for at least 3 days, shaking from time to time. Store in the freezer until ready to use.

BLACK CURRANT CURD

MAKES 2 PINTS

2 cups sugar
12 large egg yolks, lightly beaten and strained
1 cup black currant juice
1 cup (2 sticks) unsalted butter, at room temperature
2 tablespoons cassis (black currant liqueur)

Combine the sugar and egg yolks in a medium saucepan. Gradually stir in black currant juice. Cook, stirring constantly, over low heat, until mixture coats the back of a spoon and the temperature registers 168° F. on a candy thermometer. Do not allow the mixture to boil.

Remove from the heat and whisk mixture until slightly cooled. Stir in butter, 1 tablespoon at a time, and add cassis. While it is still warm, pour mixture into sterilized jars, cover tightly, and refrigerate until ready to use.

LEMON CURD

MAKES 2 PINTS

2 cups sugar
12 large egg yolks, lightly beaten and strained
1 cup lemon juice
1 cup (2 sticks) unsalted butter, at room temperature
2 tablespoons grated lemon peel

Follow the cooking directions for Black Currant Curd (see preceding recipe), stirring in the grated lemon peel at the end.

CORN RELISH

MAKES 4 PINTS

5 cups yellow corn kernels, fresh or frozen
2½ cups finely chopped onions
2 garlic cloves, finely minced
¾ cup diced red bell pepper
½ cup diced celery
1¼ cups firmly packed light brown sugar
1½ tablespoons coarse salt
2 tablespoons dry mustard
2 teaspoons mustard seeds
1½ teaspoons celery seeds
2 teaspoons turmeric
½ teaspoon cayenne pepper
2 cups cider vinegar

Combine all ingredients in a large heavy saucepan. Bring the mixture to a boil, lower the heat, and simmer for approximately 30 minutes, stirring from time to time.

Ladle into hot, sterilized jars, leaving ¼-inch space at the top, and seal.

QUINCE JELLY

MAKES 4 PINTS

12 *large, very ripe quinces*
4½ *cups sugar*
   Sprigs fresh rosemary

Peel, core, and slice the quinces, place in a large pot, and add water to cover. Bring to a boil, and simmer 45 minutes, or until fruit is tender, adding more water to keep up level. Pour quince and liquid into a jelly bag and allow juice to drip into a bowl.

Measure 6 cups of juice into a large heavy-bottomed pot and bring to a boil over medium heat. Add sugar, stir to dissolve, and raise heat to high. Continue to stir while mixture boils.

Approximately 3 to 4 minutes after adding the sugar, begin to test syrup. When drops form and hang from a spoon (the "sheeting" stage) the jelly is done.

Remove jelly from heat and skim foam. Pour into hot, sterilized jars, add sprigs of rosemary, and seal.

HOPI CORN JAM

MAKES 4 PINTS

2 *cups corn kernels, fresh or frozen*
  Pinch of salt
5 *cups sugar*
1½ *cups cider vinegar*
1 *red bell pepper, finely diced*
1 *fresh jalapeño pepper, finely diced*
6 *ounces liquid pectin*

Place the corn kernels in a pot with the salt and enough water to cover. Bring to a boil, then simmer for 6 minutes. Drain and

return corn to the pot with all remaining ingredients except the pectin. Bring to a rolling boil, add the pectin, and continue to boil for 1 minute.

Remove jam from heat, pour into hot, sterilized jars, and seal.

PRICKLY PEAR JELLY

MAKES 3 PINTS

8–10 *prickly pears, washed and sliced crosswise*
 ½ *cup water*
 ½ *cup lime juice*
 1 *package powdered fruit pectin*
 5 *cups sugar*
   Zest of 1 lime

Place the fruit in a saucepan with the water. Bring to a simmer, then cover and cook for 20 to 30 minutes.

Mash the fruit and pour mixture into a cheesecloth or jelly bag. Allow juice to stand for at least 1 hour until sediment settles to the bottom. Discard the pulp, pour off the clear liquid and reserve, and discard the cloudy sediment.

Combine the prickly pear liquid, lime juice, and pectin in a saucepan. Bring to a boil over high heat, stirring constantly. Add the sugar and lime zest. Bring to a rolling boil, stirring constantly for 2½ minutes. Remove from heat, skim, pour into sterilized jars, and seal.

PURPLE BASIL JELLY

MAKES 2 PINTS

1½ *cups packed purple basil, washed and dried*
   Zest of 1 lemon
 3 *whole cloves*
 2 *allspice berries*
1¾ *cups orange juice*
 ½ *cup balsamic vinegar*
 4 *cups sugar*
 3 *ounces liquid pectin*

Crush the basil leaves with your hands and place in a saucepan. Add the lemon zest, cloves, allspice, orange juice, and vinegar, then bring slowly to a boil. Transfer to a bowl, cover, and let stand for at least 30 minutes.

Strain the mixture through a fine sieve, pressing to extract all juices. Measure 2 cups of extracted liquid into a saucepan. Add the sugar and bring to a boil. Stir in the pectin and boil for 1 minute. Remove from heat, skim, pour into hot, sterilized jars, and seal.

HERB-GARDEN VINEGAR

MAKES 1 QUART

4 *sprigs fresh thyme*
4 *sprigs fresh rosemary*
2 *large garlic cloves, peeled*
1 *quart Champagne vinegar*

Add thyme, rosemary, and garlic cloves to a container of vinegar and close tightly. Allow to sit for at least a week before using.

Opposite: Before we pack up our food baskets, each jar is "wrapped" with a topping of pretty fabric and ribbon.

SPICED SECKEL PEARS

MAKES 4 QUARTS

- 6 cups distilled white vinegar
- 8 cups loosely packed light brown sugar
- 1 tablespoon ground cloves
- 1 stick cinnamon
- 1 tablespoon juniper berries
- 6 hot red peppers
- 6 pounds seckel pears

Place all ingredients except the pears into a large heavy-bottomed pot. Cook over medium heat until the brown sugar has melted, about 5 minutes.

Peel the pears, leaving the stems on, and place them in the pot with the vinegar mixture. Bring to a boil, then reduce the heat and simmer until pears are tender, about 10 minutes.

Pack the hot pears into hot sterilized jars, cover with the boiling liquid to within ½ inch of jars' tops, and seal.

Opposite: Spiced seckel pears can be packed in sterilized, sealed jars. The high vinegar content of the liquid makes it unnecessary to process these pears, but it is important to create a perfect seal by wiping the jars and lids absolutely clean before tightening. Stored in a cool, dry place they will keep almost forever and are a delicious accompaniment to roast duck.

PEAR CHUTNEY

MAKES 4 PINTS

- 2 pounds ripe, firm pears, peeled, cored, and diced
- 1 cup cider vinegar
- 1 cup packed light brown sugar
- 1 cup diced onion
- 1 tablespoon minced garlic
- 1 tablespoon minced fresh ginger
- 1 tablespoon minced fresh chile pepper
- 1 cup dried cherries
  Salt and ground black pepper

Combine all ingredients in a noncorroding pot. Bring to a boil, reduce heat, and simmer for 30 minutes, stirring occasionally. Season with salt and pepper. Pour into hot, sterilized jars and seal.

ONION CHUTNEY

MAKES 1½ PINTS

- 2 cups pearl onions
- ¼ cup finely minced garlic
- ⅓ cup balsamic vinegar
- ⅓ cup olive oil
- ⅓ cup golden raisins
- ¼ cup catsup
- ¼ cup packed light brown sugar
  Salt and ground black pepper

Cut a little x in the root end of each onion, cover with water, and bring to a boil. Drain, drop into cold water, and pinch onions to remove outer skins.

Mix all ingredients in a heavy saucepan, cover, and simmer, stirring occasionally, for 1 hour. Uncover pot and continue cooking until onions are soft and glazed, about 30 minutes. Season with salt and pepper. Pour into hot, sterilized jars and seal.

NO-MEAT MINCEMEAT

MAKES 8 PINTS

- 3 quarts chopped green tomatoes
- 2 tablespoons coarse salt
- 2 oranges
- 2 lemons
- 1 quart slightly underripe pears, peeled, cored, and diced
- 1½ quarts tart apples, peeled, cored, and diced
- 2 cups dark raisins
- 1½ teaspoons ground cinnamon
- 1 teaspoon ground allspice
- 1 teaspoon ground cloves
- ¼ cup finely chopped fresh ginger
- ½ cup cider vinegar
- ½ cup frozen apple-juice concentrate
- 1 pound light brown sugar
- ¾ cup cognac

Mix the green tomatoes and salt. Place in a colander and allow to drain overnight.

Using a citrus stripper, remove the bright colored skin from the oranges and lemons and reserve. With a sharp knife, cut away the white pith and discard. Chop the pulp coarsely.

Combine the tomatoes, citrus peel, and pulp with the remaining ingredients except cognac in a heavy noncorroding saucepan and bring to a boil. Reduce heat and simmer, uncovered, for about 2 hours, stirring frequently to prevent sticking.

Stir cognac into mincemeat, ladle into hot, sterilized canning jars, and seal.

Of course there were sweets. It was the marshmallows that squelched. Hardboileds, toffee, fudge and allsorts, crunches, cracknels, humbugs, glaciers, and marzipan and butterwelsh for the Welsh.

Dylan Thomas

In the house where I grew up, cookie baking started weeks before Christmas, and it was an activity enjoyed by everyone in our large family. We loved mixing up great big batches of flavorful cookie doughs; forming the cookies by hand, cutter, or press; baking them on heavy sheets; and then decorating them with melted chocolate, lemony royal icing, or colored sugars. We soon discovered who was the best dough maker (before we got our big mixer, only the strongest could beat up large amounts of dough), the best roller, or the best decorator. Mother taught us to make a game of the entire process, and the house was filled with laughter as conversation and storytelling helped to pass the hours.

The tradition of cookie making has contin-ued as we all grew up and had our own families. Our spouses' favorite recipes have been incorporated into our repertoire, and the number of cookies made, instead of diminishing, has actually increased. After all these years, cookie making is still our favorite task.

Opposite: Golds, coppers, bronzes, and silvery shades were our Christmas colors this year. Even the cutout cookie ornaments for a boxwood topiary were covered with shiny copper leaf.

Above: An interior view of the "Palais de Poulets," our daily source of fresh, rich eggs. I have become quite spoiled by these eggs; they make a great difference to my cooking and baking.

MELISSA'S GINGERBREAD COOKIES

MAKES 3 TO 4 DOZEN

- 1 *cup dark molasses*
- ½ *cup light brown sugar*
- ½ *cup granulated sugar*
- 4 *teaspoons ground ginger*
- 4 *teaspoons ground cinnamon*
- ¾ *tablespoon baking soda*
- 1 *cup (2 sticks) unsalted butter, at room temperature*
- 2 *large eggs, lightly beaten*
- 6 *cups sifted all-purpose flour*

ROYAL ICING
- 1 *cup sifted confectioners' sugar*
- 1 *large egg white*
  Food coloring

Place the molasses, sugar, ginger, and cinnamon in a double boiler over medium heat. When the sugar has melted, add the baking soda and stir. When the mixture bubbles up, remove from heat.

Place butter in a large mixing bowl. Add the hot molasses mixture and stir well. Let mixture cool to about 90° F., then add the egg. Gradually add the flour, 1 cup at a time, while beating. (This is best done in an electric mixer, but you can use a wooden spoon.)

Preheat the oven to 325° F. and line thick baking sheets with parchment paper.

Shape the dough into a neat rectangle, place on a well-floured board, and roll out until ¼ inch thick. Cut into shapes, place shapes on the baking sheets, and bake for 15 to 20 minutes, or until firm to the touch. Let cool on racks.

Mix the confectioners' sugar and egg white; divide among small bowls and tint each a different color. Spread or pipe onto the cooled cookies and allow to set.

GINGERBREAD ORNAMENTS

MAKES 3 TO 4 DOZEN

- 1 *batch Melissa's Gingerbread Cookie dough (above)*
- 1 *batch Royal Icing (above)*

Preheat the oven to 300° F. and line thick baking sheets with parchment paper.

On a well-floured board, roll out the dough until ½ inch thick. Cut into shapes and, with a wooden or metal skewer, form a hole in each shape for threading with ribbon or raffia. Place on baking sheets and bake 30 minutes, or until thoroughly dry. Let cool on racks, then decorate with Royal Icing.

SPATTERWARE COOKIES

1. I love the traditional American pottery called "spatterware," and thought it would be fun to create cookies with the same look. Using Melissa's gingerbread as the base, we first glazed each cookie with a thin coating of white royal icing and allowed them to dry.

2. We mixed up thin batches of bright-colored royal icing for the spatter, and, with a piece of natural sponge, applied one color to each glazed cookie.

3. For this old fashioned decoration, we found that domestic or rustic cookie shapes—like the pig, heart, pitcher, and rooster—worked best.

Opposite: When decorating cookies or cakes, it is important to have the icing exactly the right consistency for each task. If raised dots or a lacy effect are desired, the icing must be quite stiff; to make lines or a coating, add a bit more egg white for a thinner icing.

COPPER COOKIE TREE

1. To decorate my parlor, I made a boxwood topiary by sticking small branches of box into a grapevine-covered cone of heavy wire. (You could also fashion such a cone from chicken or rabbit wire, but take care not to leave any scratchy metal exposed.)

2. Cookie ornaments were created from Melissa's gingerbread, then brushed with softly beaten egg white. Copper leaf (see note) was then carefully applied to each cookie and gently patted with a soft cloth to make it adhere well.

3. The coppered cookies were then hung amid the boxwood with little "s" hooks, which we fabricated from heavy florist's wire, and the completed tree was placed on my 18th-century tilt-top table in the parlor.

NOTE: *I get my metal leaf—copper, gold, or silver—from Sepp Leaf Products in New York City. All must be handled with care, especially the gold leaf, which is so thin it is the most difficult to apply. Most good art-supply stores carry metal leaf, or they can order it for you in small quantities. (Gold leaf of at least 23 karats is edible, as is silver leaf. Copper is not.)*

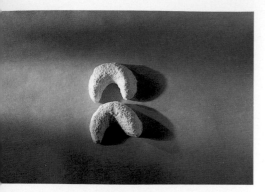

Top: Almond crescents are similar to those made with pecans, but smaller and daintier.

Middle: If these anise cookies are to puff properly, you must sift the flour, use an electric mixer (they must be beaten for 30 minutes), and let them dry at least 10 hours before baking.

Above: As a child, I made jewel cookies like these with red and green candied cherries in the center. Now I use a bit of red raspberry jam.

ALMOND CRESCENTS

MAKES 3 DOZEN

    1 cup (2 sticks) unsalted butter
   ⅔ cup sifted confectioners' sugar, plus
       extra for rolling
    1 teaspoon vanilla extract
   ½ teaspoon almond extract
    1 cup coarsely chopped almonds
  2⅓ cups sifted all-purpose flour

Cream the butter and the ⅔ cup confectioners' sugar until fluffy. Beat in the vanilla and almond extracts, then add the almonds. Stir in the flour and beat until well mixed.

Preheat the oven to 350° F. and line baking sheets with parchment paper.

Divide the dough in half and form each half into a roll 1 inch in diameter. Cut each roll into ¾-inch slices, roll each slice into a cylinder 2 inches long, place 1 to 2 inches apart on baking sheet, and form into a crescent.

Bake for 15 to 20 minutes, or until lightly golden. Let cool, then roll in confectioners' sugar.

ANISE COOKIES

MAKES 2 DOZEN

    2 large eggs
    1 cup sugar
  1¼ cups sifted all-purpose flour
    1 teaspoon anise seeds
       Anise oil (optional)
       Lemon zest (optional)

Generously butter and flour baking sheets.

Beat the eggs until frothy. Add the sugar and continue beating, at medium speed, for 30 minutes. Add the flour and the anise seeds and, if desired, a few drops of anise oil and the lemon zest. Continue to beat 5 more minutes.

Drop the batter from a teaspoon onto the baking sheets; allow 1 inch between cookies. Let stand at least 10 hours at room temperature.

Preheat the oven to 350° F. Bake 10 minutes, or until the cookies puff like meringues. Cool on racks.

JEWEL COOKIES

MAKES 5 DOZEN

  1½ cups (3 sticks) unsalted butter
    1 cup packed light brown sugar
    2 large eggs, separated
    2 teaspoons vanilla extract
   ¼ teaspoon salt
  2⅔ cups sifted all-purpose flour
    2 cups finely chopped pecans
    1 cup thick raspberry jam

Preheat the oven to 350° F. and line baking sheets with parchment paper.

Cream the butter and sugar. Beat in the egg yolks, vanilla, and salt, then the flour. Shape dough into 1-inch balls.

Brush each dough ball with beaten egg white and then roll in the chopped pecans and place 2 to 3 inches apart on baking sheets. Press the center of each ball with your thumb and fill with ½ teaspoon of jam.

Bake for 8 to 10 minutes, until just golden around the edges. Cool on rack.

SANDKAKERS

MAKES 4 DOZEN

1 cup (2 sticks) unsalted butter
¾ cup sugar
½ teaspoon vanilla extract
1 large egg, lightly beaten
2 cups sifted all-purpose flour
⅓ cup chopped blanched almonds

Preheat the oven to 375° F. and butter sandkaker or tartlet tins.

Cream the butter, sugar, and vanilla. Stir in the egg. Combine flour and almonds and add to butter mixture; beat until smooth.

Press about 2 teaspoons of dough into each tin. Place tins on a cookie sheet and bake for 6 to 8 minutes, or until golden brown. Cool in tins 4 to 5 minutes, then remove and cool on racks.

JENNIFER'S COOKIES

MAKES 2 DOZEN

1 cup (2 sticks) unsalted butter
1 cup sugar
4 large egg yolks, lightly beaten
1 tablespoon vanilla extract
2¼ cups sifted all-purpose flour
Pinch of salt
Beaten egg white
Poppy seeds

Cream the butter and sugar. Add the egg yolks and beat until fluffy. Stir in the vanilla, flour, and salt. Beat well. Form into flat rounds, wrap, and refrigerate 2 hours.

Preheat the oven to 350° F. and line baking sheets with parchment.

Roll dough ⅛ inch thick on a well-floured board. Cut into shapes and place 1 to 2 inches apart on baking sheets. Brush with the beaten egg white and sprinkle with poppy seeds.

Bake for 8 to 10 minutes, until lightly browned on the edges. Cool on a rack.

CANDY CANE COOKIES

MAKES 2 DOZEN

1 cup (2 sticks) unsalted butter
1 cup sifted confectioners' sugar
1 large egg
½ teaspoon vanilla extract
½ teaspoon peppermint extract
¼ teaspoon salt
2½ cups sifted all-purpose flour
¼ teaspoon red food coloring

Cream the butter with the confectioners' sugar until fluffy. Beat in the egg, vanilla, peppermint, salt, and flour.

Divide the dough in half. Stir the food coloring into one half. Wrap both pieces of dough and refrigerate several hours.

Preheat the oven to 350° F. and line baking sheets with parchment.

Shape a teaspoon of plain dough into a 4-inch-long cylinder. Do the same with the red dough. Twist the cylinders together and bend into a cane shape. Repeat with rest of the dough, setting canes 1 to 2 inches apart on baking sheets.

Bake for 8 to 10 minutes; do not allow to brown. Set the baking sheets on racks to cool.

Top: Sandkakers must be made in special molds, available from Scandinavian specialty stores.

Middle: Jennifer Levin often makes these cookies for holidays.

Above: Children love candy cane cookies so much we always make a couple of batches at Christmas.

Following pages: The dining-room table was laden with glass pedestals, holding our festive cookies.

Top: The sugar glaze on these crisp, chewy cinnamon cookies gives them the look of old pottery.

Above: Cookie press cookies are difficult to make—the dough seems at first too hard, too cold, too stiff, or too soft to push through the press. Then all at once it works and perfect cookies appear on the sheet. They can be baked plain, sprinkled with colored sugars, or "glued" together with melted chocolate.

CINNAMON COOKIES

MAKES 2 DOZEN

4 *large egg whites, at room temperature*
2½ *cups granulated sugar*
3 *cups finely ground blanched almonds*
4 *tablespoons ground cinnamon*
1 *tablespoon ground ginger*
1 *teaspoon ground mace*
1 *teaspoon grated nutmeg*
1 *cup sifted all-purpose flour*
2 *cups sifted confectioners' sugar*
4 *tablespoons water*

Beat the egg whites until soft peaks form. Gradually add 2 cups of granulated sugar, 2 tablespoons at a time, while still beating; egg whites will become thick and glossy.

In a large bowl, combine the ground almonds and the spices. Gently fold in the egg whites, cover, and refrigerate overnight.

The following day, line baking sheets with parchment paper. Divide the egg-white dough into four parts. Mix the flour with the remaining ½ cup of granulated sugar and sprinkle evenly over a large board. Roll one quarter of the dough out over the flour and sugar to a thickness of ¼ inch. Cut into shapes and, with a spatula, carefully lift onto the baking sheets. Continue with the remaining dough.

Allow the cut-out cookies to reach room temperature, about 1 hour, then preheat oven to 300° F. Make a glaze by mixing the confectioners' sugar and water and stirring until smooth.

Bake cookies for 35 minutes. Remove from the oven and brush with the glaze. Return cookies to oven and bake 2 more minutes. Cool on baking sheets set on racks.

COOKIE-PRESS COOKIES

MAKES 2 TO 3 DOZEN

1½ *cups (3 sticks) unsalted butter*
1 *cup sugar*
2 *large egg yolks*
3¾ *cups sifted all-purpose flour*
¼ *teaspoon salt*
1 *tablespoon vanilla extract*
6 *ounces semisweet chocolate for decoration*

Preheat the oven to 350° F.

Cream the butter and sugar until light and fluffy. Add the egg yolks, flour, salt, and vanilla. Mix thoroughly.

Fill a cookie press with the dough and turn out cookies 1 to 2 inches apart onto an unbuttered baking sheet.

Bake for 7 to 10 minutes, or until the cookies are lightly browned. Cool on a rack. Melt the chocolate, spread it on the cookie bottoms, and stick them together in pairs.

PECAN CRESCENTS

MAKES 4 DOZEN

2 cups sifted all-purpose flour
1 cup (2 sticks) unsalted butter
1 cup finely chopped pecans
½ cup sifted confectioners' sugar, plus extra for dusting
½ teaspoon salt
1 teaspoon vanilla extract
¼ teaspoon almond extract

In a large bowl, combine all the ingredients except the dusting sugar. Mix well with your hands. Wrap the dough and refrigerate for at least 2 hours.

Preheat the oven to 375° F. and line baking sheets with parchment paper.

Form the dough into 1-inch balls, then roll each ball into a 2-inch roll. Ends should be narrow and the center slightly flattened to create a crescent moon when curved. Set 1 to 2 inches apart on baking sheets.

Bake for 12 to 15 minutes, until set but not browned. Allow cookies to cool slightly on a rack, then, using a fine sieve, apply a thick dusting of confectioners' sugar.

NOËL NUT BALLS

MAKES 3 DOZEN

1 cup (2 sticks) unsalted butter
2 tablespoons honey
½ cup sifted confectioners' sugar
2¼ cups sifted all-purpose flour
¼ teaspoon salt
1 teaspoon bourbon or orange juice
¾ cup finely chopped pecans
Confectioners' sugar, for rolling

Cream the butter and honey until fluffy. Stir in the confectioners' sugar, flour, salt, bourbon or orange juice, and pecans. Wrap and refrigerate for several hours.

Preheat the oven to 350° F. and butter baking sheets.

With your hands, roll the dough, 1 teaspoon at a time, into balls. Place balls on baking sheets and bake for 12 to 13 minutes. Let cool on racks, then roll in confectioners' sugar.

LINDY'S OATMEAL CRACKERS

MAKES 4 TO 5 DOZEN

1 cup (2 sticks) unsalted butter
2 cups quick-cooking oats
2 cups sifted all-purpose flour
1 cup packed dark brown sugar
½ teaspoon salt
½ teaspoon baking soda
½ teaspoon baking powder
¼ cup boiling water

Melt the butter. Mix the dry ingredients, add the butter, mix thoroughly, then add the water. Refrigerate until firm, about 4 hours.

Preheat the oven to 350° F. and line baking sheets with parchment paper.

On a floured board, roll out the dough until ¼ to ⅛ inch thick and cut into 2-inch rounds. Place 1 to 2 inches apart on baking sheets; leftover dough can be rolled and cut once more.

Bake for 10 minutes; do not allow crackers to become too brown. Cool on baking sheets.

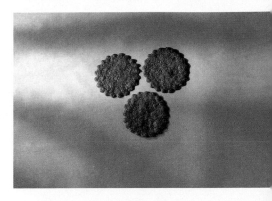

Top: I got this recipe for pecan crescents from Miss Baer, my home economics teacher in junior high school.

Middle: Lindy, Rita's aunt, brought this oatmeal cracker recipe from Norway; she taught us to roll the dough very thin, and to store the fragile cookies in an airtight tin.

Above: When I first brought Andy home for Christmas, my brothers teased us by replacing my buttery Noël nut balls with plaster fakes.

Not strictly cookies, but so delicious we had to include them, our homemade marshmallows are cut into heart shapes with a cookie cutter, then dipped in confectioners' sugar. They must be kept in a sealed container, and are best eaten within two days of their making.

MARTHA'S MARSHMALLOWS

4 envelopes unflavored gelatin
1½ cups water
3 cups sugar
1¼ cups light corn syrup
¼ teaspoon salt
2 teaspoons vanilla extract
1½ cups confectioners' sugar, plus additional for rolling

Oil a 3-quart Pyrex baking dish with vegetable oil. Line the dish with lightweight aluminum foil, and lightly coat the foil with more oil.

In the bowl of an electric mixer, soften the gelatin with ¾ cup water.

Place the sugar, corn syrup, ¾ cup water, and the salt in a heavy saucepan. Bring to a boil and cook over high heat until the syrup reaches 234 to 240° F., or the soft-ball stage, on a candy thermometer.

With the whisk attachment of the mixer at full speed, beat the hot syrup slowly into the gelatin until mixture is very stiff, about 15 minutes. Pour the mixture into the foil-lined dish and smooth the top with an oiled spatula. Allow the mixture to rest, uncovered, at room temperature 10 to 12 hours.

Using a fine sieve, sprinkle the confectioner's sugar onto a cutting board. Turn the stiffened marshmallow mixture out onto the sugar, and using a lightly oiled cookie cutter, cut into shapes. Be sure to dip the cut edges of the marshmallows into confectioners' sugar to prevent sticking.

SUGAR COOKIES

MAKES 2 DOZEN

- ½ cup (1 stick) unsalted butter
- 1 cup granulated sugar
- 2 cups sifted all-purpose flour
- ¼ teaspoon salt
- ½ teaspoon baking powder
- 1 large egg, lightly beaten
- 2 tablespoons brandy
- ½ teaspoon vanilla extract

ROYAL ICING

- 1 cup confectioners' sugar
- 1 egg white
  Food coloring

Cream the butter and sugar. Sift together the dry ingredients; add to the butter mixture and beat well. Add the egg, brandy, and vanilla and beat again until well mixed. Shape dough into two flattened rounds, wrap, and refrigerate at least 1 hour.

Preheat the oven to 350° F. and line baking sheets with parchment.

On a well-floured board, roll out the dough until ⅛ inch thick. Cut into shapes and set 1 to 2 inches apart on baking sheets. Leftover dough can be rolled and cut once more.

Bake for about 10 minutes; do not allow to brown. Cool on racks.

Mix the confectioners' sugar and egg white; divide among small bowls and tint each a different color. Spread or pipe onto the cooled cookies and allow to set.

Top: Sugar cookie dough is just the right consistency for making intricate cutout cookies. I have a huge variety of cookie cutters and I am forever adding new shapes from cookware stores, catalogues, or antiques shops. Even so, I sometimes make my own cookie shapes by cutting out cardboard forms, then cutting cookie dough around them.

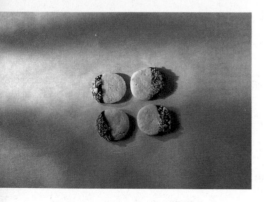

Top: Chocolate pepper cookie dough is easily cut into complicated shapes.

Middle: Appliqué cookies are made by applying sugar cookie dough to chocolate pepper dough, or vice versa.

Above: Chocolate-dipped almond cookies are wonderful for tea parties.

Opposite: Using a small round frosting tip and some good, melted semisweet chocolate, I squiggled lines over these appliqué cookies.

CHOCOLATE PEPPER COOKIES

MAKES 3 TO 4 DOZEN

1½ cups (3 sticks) unsalted butter
1¾ cups sugar
  2 large eggs, lightly beaten
  3 cups sifted all-purpose flour
1½ cups unsweetened cocoa powder
  ¼ teaspoon salt
  ⅓ teaspoon freshly ground black pepper
    Pinch of cayenne pepper
  1 teaspoon ground cinnamon
4–6 ounces semisweet chocolate, for decoration

Cream the butter and sugar. Add the eggs and beat until fluffy. Sift together the dry ingredients. Add to the butter mixture and beat until well mixed; if dough seems too soft, add up to ¼ cup more flour. Shape into a flattened round, wrap, and refrigerate at least 1 hour.

Preheat the oven to 350° F. and line baking sheets with parchment paper.

On a well-floured board, roll out the dough until ⅛ inch thick. (It's best to divide and roll out a quarter or third of the dough at a time, leaving the remainder in the refrigerator.) Cut dough into shapes and set 1 to 2 inches apart on baking sheets. Leftover dough can be rolled and cut once more.

Bake for 8 to 10 minutes, or just until crisp; do not allow to darken. Cool on racks.

Melt the chocolate and drizzle over the cooled cookies in a haphazard fashion; allow to harden completely before serving.

APPLIQUÉ COOKIES

MAKES 2 DOZEN

1 recipe Chocolate Pepper Cookie dough (see preceding recipe)
1 recipe Sugar Cookie dough (page 47)
  Beaten egg white

Roll out each dough until ⅛ inch thick. (Since these cookies will not be frosted, you may want to do the rolling on a sugar-sprinkled board.) With cookie cutters or cardboard forms, cut cookie shapes of different sizes from each dough.

Preheat the oven to 350° F. and line baking sheets with parchment paper.

With a pastry brush, coat the underside of the smaller cookies with egg-white "glue"; place on top of contrasting-color larger cookies. Set 1 to 2 inches apart on baking sheets.

Bake for 8 to 10 minutes; do not allow to brown. Cool on racks.

CHOCOLATE-DIPPED ALMOND COOKIES

MAKES 6 DOZEN

- 1 cup (2 sticks) unsalted butter
- 2/3 cup sugar
- 1 large egg yolk
- 1 teaspoon vanilla extract
- 2 cups sifted all-purpose flour
- 1/4 teaspoon salt
- 1 1/3 cups finely chopped blanched almonds

FOR DECORATION

- 6 ounces semisweet chocolate
- 3 tablespoons unsalted butter
- 1 tablespoon hot water
  Chopped almonds, for garnish

Cream the butter and sugar until light and fluffy. Add the egg yolk and vanilla, then the flour, salt, and finely chopped almonds, mixing well.

Shape the dough into 2 rolls, each 1 1/2 inches in diameter. Wrap rolls and refrigerate until firm, about 2 hours.

Preheat the oven to 350° F. and line baking sheets with parchment paper.

With a sharp knife, cut the dough into 1/4-inch-thick slices. Place 1 to 2 inches apart on baking sheets and bake for 8 to 10 minutes, just until lightly browned. Cool on a rack.

In the top of a double boiler, melt the chocolate and butter for the topping. Add the hot water and stir until smooth. Dip an edge of each cookie into the chocolate, then sprinkle with the chopped almonds. Cool on a rack until the chocolate hardens.

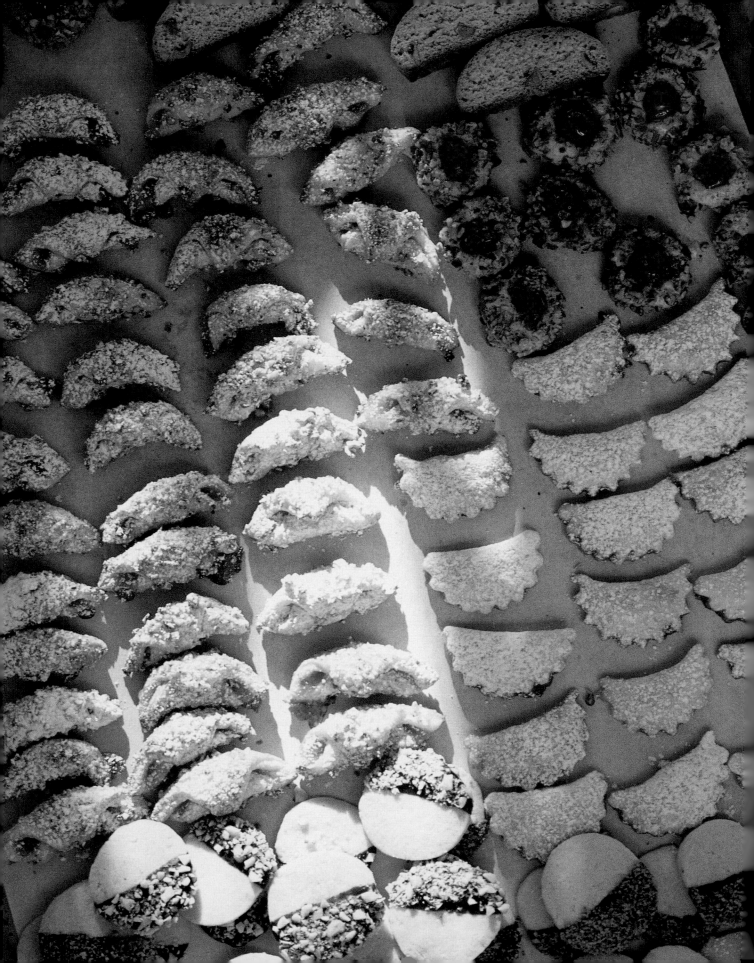

HUNGARIAN FILLED COOKIES

MAKES 2 DOZEN

½ cup (1 stick) unsalted butter
1 tablespoon lard
2 cups sifted all-purpose flour
¼ teaspoon salt
3 small egg yolks
½ cup sour cream
½ cup guava jelly
2 tablespoons milk
  Confectioners' sugar, for
  sprinkling

In a large bowl, combine the butter, lard, flour, and salt. Cut with a pastry blender or work with your fingertips until the mixture has the consistency of cornmeal. Drop in 2 egg yolks, add the sour cream, and mix thoroughly. Wrap and refrigerate overnight.

Preheat the oven to 400° F. and butter baking sheets.

On a lightly floured board, roll out the dough until ⅛ inch thick. Cut into 3-inch rounds. Place about ½ teaspoon guava jelly off center on each round. Fold the dough, completely covering the jelly, and press the edges to seal; place 2 to 3 inches apart on baking sheets. Beat together the remaining egg yolk and the milk; brush this glaze onto the crescents.

Bake for 10 to 12 minutes, or until golden. Remove from sheets while still warm and cool on racks. Sprinkle with confectioners' sugar.

HAZELNUT BISCOTTI

MAKES 4 DOZEN

1 cup hazelnuts
½ cup (1 stick) unsalted butter
¾ cup sugar
1 tablespoon grated lemon peel
3 large eggs
1 teaspoon vanilla extract
3 cups sifted all-purpose flour
1 tablespoon baking powder
1 teaspoon salt

Preheat the oven to 350° F.

Place the hazelnuts on a baking sheet and toast lightly in the oven about 15 to 18 minutes, shaking the pan occasionally. Remove the nuts from the oven and roll in a clean dish towel, rubbing the skins off. Coarsely chop the skinned nuts.

Cream the butter, sugar, and lemon peel until fluffy. Add the eggs, one at a time, beating well. Stir in the vanilla. Sift the dry ingredients together and gradually add to the butter mixture, combining thoroughly. Stir in the chopped nuts.

Divide the dough into three equal pieces. Shape each piece into a 2- to 2½-inch-diameter log. Place logs on a parchment-lined baking sheet and press down to form a flattened arch shape.

Bake for 15 minutes. Remove from the oven and, with a very sharp knife, cut flattened logs into ¾-inch slices. Lay the slices on their sides 1 to 2 inches apart on the baking sheet, return to the oven, and continue baking until biscotti are dry and lightly browned, approximately 15 minutes more. Cool on a rack.

VIENNA TARTS

MAKES 18

½ cup (1 stick) unsalted butter
3 ounces cream cheese
1 cup sifted all-purpose flour
¼ cup apricot jam
1 large egg yolk
2 tablespoons milk
¼ cup finely chopped walnuts
  Confectioners' sugar, for
  sprinkling

Cream the butter and cream cheese until fluffy. Add the flour and knead until smooth. Wrap and refrigerate for at least 3 hours.

Preheat the oven to 400° F. and butter baking sheets.

Roll out the dough until ⅛ inch thick and cut into 2-inch squares. Place ¼ teaspoon jam in one corner of each square. Fold square to completely cover the jam, press down to seal, and roll diagonally. Place on cookie sheets and form into crescents.

Beat together the egg yolk and milk; brush this glaze onto the crescents and sprinkle with chopped nuts. Bake for 12 to 15 minutes, or until golden. Let cool on racks, then sprinkle with confectioners' sugar.

Opposite: These cookies were just taken out of the oven. We cool them by simply pulling the parchment paper carefully from the pan and placing it, cookies and all, on a rack.

PECAN SHORTBREAD COOKIES

MAKES 2 DOZEN

- 1 cup (2 sticks) unsalted butter
- 1 cup loosely packed light brown sugar
- 1/2 teaspoon vanilla extract
  Pinch of salt
- 2 1/4 cups sifted cake flour
- 1/2 cup finely chopped pecans

Beat together the butter, brown sugar, vanilla, and salt. Add the flour, then the nuts. Gather the dough into a ball and flatten into a circle between 2 pieces of floured plastic wrap. Refrigerate at least 30 minutes.

Preheat the oven to 325° F. and line baking sheets with parchment paper.

Roll out the dough on a lightly floured board until 1/4 inch thick and cut into shapes. Set 1 to 2 inches apart on baking sheets; leftover dough can be rolled and cut once more. Bake in top third of the oven for 20 minutes—just until edges are golden—then cool on racks.

Opposite: After the cookies have cooled they are packed in rigid plastic containers with tight-fitting lids, and can be stored in a cool place for up to a week, or in the freezer for up to a month.

MORAVIAN MOLASSES COOKIES

MAKES 7 DOZEN

- 1 1/4 cups firmly packed light brown sugar
- 6 tablespoons (3/4 stick) margarine
- 6 tablespoons solid vegetable shortening
- 2 cups dark molasses
- 1 tablespoon baking soda
- 1/4 cup boiling water
- 6 2/3 cups sifted all-purpose flour
- 1 tablespoon ground cloves
- 2 tablespoons ground ginger
- 1 tablespoon ground cinnamon

In a heavy saucepan, combine the brown sugar, margarine, vegetable shortening, and molasses. Heat until brown sugar is dissolved.

Dissolve the baking soda in the boiling water and stir into the molasses mixture. The mixture will bubble up. Remove from heat.

Sift the flour and spices together and gradually add to the saucepan, stirring with a wooden spoon until well incorporated. Form the dough into a rectangle, wrap, and let set overnight. Do not refrigerate.

The next day, preheat the oven to 275° F. and line baking sheets with parchment paper.

On a floured board, roll small pieces of dough as thin as possible. (Dough should be thin enough to see one's hand through it.) Cut with cookie cutter and set 1 to 2 inches apart on baking sheet. Bake for exactly 10 minutes and allow to cool on baking sheets.

SCOTCH SHORTBREAD

MAKES 1 GIANT COOKIE

> 1 cup (2 sticks) unsalted butter
> ¼ pound sugar
> 1 pound sifted all-purpose flour

Preheat the oven to 350° F. Butter an 8-inch round baking tin and line bottom with parchment paper.

Cream the butter and sugar. Add the flour and mix well; the mixture will be very crumbly.

Pack the mixture into the tin, smoothing the top with a rubber scraper. Mark the top with a decorative pattern (we used a butter knife and the tines of a fork).

Bake for about 25 minutes; do not allow to brown. Cool 10 minutes in tin, then turn onto rack.

Scotch shortbread was one of the first baked goods we gave as a Christmas gift. I made eight-inch shortbreads, decorated them before baking with knife lines and the tines of a fork, placed them atop antique English breadboards, wrapped them in clear cellophane, and tied them with deep burgundy ribbons. It was such a successful presentation, we have not altered it much over the years—though this Christmas we used golden yellow ribbons and gilded galax leaves and holly for the wrappings. For fun, we also made some shortbreads in unusual shapes, baking them in antique scallop-shell candy molds.

Mary and Laura pulled out two small packages.
They unwrapped them, and each found a little heart-shaped cake.
Over their delicate brown tops was sprinkled white sugar.
The sparkling grains lay like tiny drifts of snow.

Laura Ingalls Wilder

Our family tradition of cake baking began when I was a very young child in Nutley, New Jersey, in the amazing basement kitchen of Mr. and Mrs. Maus, retired German bakers of great repute and girth. Yeast cakes were their specialty, and Christmas was their favorite season.

The Mauses were great teachers and generous with their baked goods, recipes, and ideas. They taught us that even in baking, attention to detail will ensure the most flavorful results. Raisins, candied fruits, nuts, and citrus juices must be as fresh as possible. Good unsalted butter and high-quality unbleached flour; warm kitchens and even-temperature ovens; heavy tins and parchment-covered baking sheets all contribute greatly to the success of the finished product.

Everyone in my family learned so much about baking from Mr. and Mrs. Maus that each of us can make pastry, breads, and cakes that rival —if they don't equal—theirs.

Opposite: The baba au rhum was surrounded by fresh red currants (from New Zealand), and crowned with whipped cream; it fit beautifully on my footed silver tray.

Above: Some of my puffy spring-steel garden chairs were left on the terrace, where they grew snow "cushions."

BABA AU RHUM

MAKES TWO 9-INCH CAKES

- 2 *packages active dry yeast*
- 1 *cup warm milk*
- ½ *cup plus 1 teaspoon sugar*
- 8 *large eggs, lightly beaten*
- 4 *cups sifted all-purpose flour*
- 1 *teaspoon salt*
- 1½ *cups (3 sticks) unsalted butter*
     Fresh berries and whipped cream,
     for garnish

Butter a large bowl and set aside. Proof the yeast in the warm milk with the teaspoon of sugar. Combine the eggs with the flour and beat until smooth. Add the yeast mixture and knead for 5 minutes. (This may be done with an electric mixer equipped with a dough hook.) Transfer dough to the buttered bowl, cover with plastic wrap, and let rise until doubled in bulk, about 1 hour.

Punch dough down and add the remaining ½ cup of sugar and the salt. Knead the dough in the bowl by cupping your hand and vigorously slapping the dough against the side of the bowl. Incorporate the butter 1 stick at a time in this manner. When all the butter has been added, continue kneading by hand for approximately 5 minutes. Dough will remain very sticky.

Preheat the oven to 400° F. and butter two 9-inch savarin molds. Fill molds halfway with the dough. Put in a warm place and allow dough to rise to just below the top of the mold, about 1 hour. Bake for 10 minutes, reduce the heat to 350° F., and continue baking until babas are golden brown and pulling away from the sides of the molds, about 25 to 30 minutes more.

Remove from the oven and allow the cakes to cool in the pan for 5 minutes. Invert onto racks.

To serve, brush babas with Rum Syrup (see recipe below) and garnish with fresh berries and whipped cream.

RUM SYRUP

MAKES 1½ CUPS

- 1 *cup water*
- 1 *cup sugar*
- ½ *cup light rum*

Bring water and sugar to a boil. Remove from the heat and stir in the rum.

PERSIMMON PUDDING

SERVES 12

3 large very ripe persimmons
½ cup sugar
6 tablespoons vegetable oil
4 large eggs
2 teaspoons vanilla extract
2 cups all-purpose flour
1 teaspoon baking soda
½ teaspoon salt
2 teaspoons ground cinnamon

Oil a 3-quart pudding mold or baking dish with vegetable oil.

Peel the persimmons and mash the flesh, removing black seeds (you should have about 2 cups of pulp). In a large bowl, beat together the sugar, oil, eggs, and vanilla until fluffy, then add the persimmon pulp. Sift together the flour, baking soda, salt, and cinnamon. Add to the persimmon mixture and mix just until smooth.

Pour the mixture into the pudding mold and cover tightly with a round of parchment paper and a rubber band, then with foil. Place on a rack in a large pot and add boiling water until it comes halfway up the mold. Cover the pot, bring water to a boil, then reduce heat and simmer for 2½ hours, adding boiling water as necessary to maintain level.

Remove mold from pot and uncover pudding; the top should spring back when touched. Cool pudding for one hour, then run a sharp knife around the top edge of the pudding to loosen from the mold and invert carefully onto a serving platter. Serve with Sour Lemon Sauce (recipe follows).

SOUR LEMON SAUCE

MAKES 2 CUPS

1 cup sugar
1¼ tablespoons cornstarch
Pinch of salt
1¼ cups hot water
3½ tablespoons unsalted butter
4 tablespoons fresh lemon juice
3 teaspoons grated lemon rind

Combine the sugar, cornstarch, and salt in the top of a double boiler. Add the hot water and cook for 3 to 5 minutes, whisking gently, until thick. Add the butter, lemon juice, and rind and continue cooking, stirring gently, for about 5 minutes. Cool slightly before using, but do not refrigerate (the sauce will become aspiclike) and do not reheat.

Far left: We baked the babas in two different shapes—a traditional savarin mold, and a more decorative turban mold. The molds must be well buttered and dusted with flour before the batter is put in for its final rise.

Left: To soak the babas with the rum syrup, place them on racks on top of baking sheets. Brush the warm syrup onto the cakes; the excess will be caught and can be used again. It is important to soak the cakes very well, and as close to serving time as possible.

Above: Persimmons are only in season for a short time, but I enjoy them to the fullest when they are available. This pudding is dense, dark, and seems rich, but there is no butter, and only a bit of sugar, in it. I serve it with sour lemon sauce (a little sweeter than the version I made in Entertaining) and a garnish of candied lemon peel.

POPPYSEED ROLL

2 packages active dry yeast
½ cup warm water
½ cup (1 stick) unsalted butter
½ cup sour cream
1 teaspoon vanilla extract
2 large eggs plus 2 egg yolks,
   lightly beaten
4½ cups all-purpose flour
¾ cup sugar
½ teaspoon salt

FILLING
1 cup dried currants
¼ cup cognac
4 tablespoons (½ stick) unsalted
   butter
1½ pounds ground poppy seeds
   (see note)
½ cup honey
   Juice of 1 lemon
4 large egg whites
1 cup sugar

EGG WASH
2 large egg yolks
1 tablespoon water

Dissolve the yeast in the warm water. Melt the butter. Sift the dry ingredients together.

In the bowl of an electric mixer, combine the yeast, melted butter, sour cream, vanilla, eggs, and egg yolks. Sift the dry ingredients, add to the yeast mixture, and stir until well blended. Knead with a dough hook or with your hands on a floured board until smooth and elastic. Place in a buttered bowl, cover with plastic wrap, and allow to rise in a warm place until doubled in bulk, approximately 1 hour.

Meanwhile, soak the currants in the cognac. In a large heavy skillet, melt the butter. Add the poppy seeds and sauté for a few

minutes, being careful not to burn. Transfer to a large bowl and add the honey, lemon juice, and currants.

In the bowl of an electric mixer, whip the egg whites until frothy. Add the sugar 1 tablespoon at a time and continue whipping until very stiff. Fold the egg whites into the poppyseed mixture.

On a floured board, roll the dough into a rectangle approximately 26 x 17 inches. Spread the filling evenly on the rectangle, leaving a 1-inch margin on the two short sides and one long side. Using a soft pastry brush, wet the margins with water and roll up the rectangle, beginning with the long edge without the margin. Form into a crescent shape, sealing the edges together, and place on a parchment-lined baking sheet. Cover with plastic wrap and allow to rise approximately 1 hour in a warm place.

Preheat the oven to 350° F. Mix egg wash.

Just before baking, brush on the egg wash. Using a serrated knife, make decorative slits in the top. Bake for 45 to 60 minutes, until deep golden brown. Cool on a rack.

NOTE: *You can grind the poppy seeds in a food grinder or purchase them already ground in gourmet or specialty shops.*

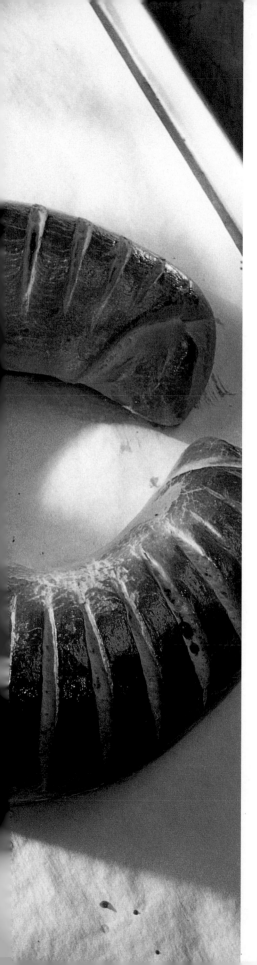

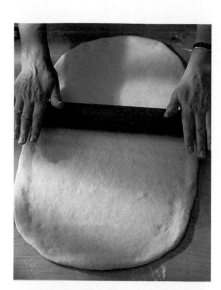

Top left: The yeast dough for our poppy seed roll is light but tasty, enriched with sour cream and egg yolks.

Middle left: I don't like to skimp on the poppy seed mixture: the baked roll should have more filling than cake.

Bottom left: The edges of the dough are moistened with a bit of water before rolling; this helps to seal the ends closed.

Far left: The baked poppy seed roll—all shiny and bronzed. The slits are made after the cake is glazed and before it is baked; they are decorative, and also prevent the cake from splitting during baking.

SOUR LEMON CAKE

   1 cup (2 sticks) unsalted butter
1½ cups sugar
   4 large eggs
   3 cups sifted all-purpose flour
   2 teaspoons baking powder
   ½ teaspoon salt
   1 cup milk
     Grated rind of 2 lemons

GLAZE
   ⅓ cup cognac
   ⅓ cup lemon juice
   ½ cup sugar

Preheat the oven to 350° F. and butter and flour the cake pan.

Cream the butter and sugar; beat in the eggs, one at a time. Sift together the flour, baking powder, and salt and add to the butter mixture, alternating with the milk. Stir in the lemon rind.

Pour batter into the pan. Bake for 1 hour, or until a tester comes out clean. Remove from the oven and allow to sit in the pan for a few minutes.

Turn the cake onto a rack. Stir the glaze ingredients together until the sugar dissolves and brush onto the cake. Allow to cool.

Opposite above: My big yellowware bowl was just large enough for the stollen.

Opposite below: Two long, flat stollen during their last rising.

Following pages: Our Christmas fruitcake is made in the traditional 8-inch round; sour lemon cakes can be made large, or in small decorative molds (if making the smaller cakes, bake for only 30 to 40 minutes).

STOLLEN

MAKES 2 CAKES

  11 cups sifted all-purpose flour
   ¾ cup sugar
   1 teaspoon salt
   ½ teaspoon ground mace
   ½ teaspoon grated nutmeg
   2 cups warm milk
1¼ cups (2½ sticks) unsalted butter, melted
   2 ounces cake yeast or 3 packages active dry yeast dissolved in ½ cup warm water
   6 large eggs, lightly beaten
  10 ounces currants, soaked in ½ cup cognac
  15 ounces golden raisins, soaked in ½ cup orange juice
   ½ pound diced citron
   ¼ pound diced orange peel
   ¼ pound chopped dried apricots
  10 ounces blanched almonds, coarsely chopped
     Grated rind of 2 lemons
     Melted butter (1 stick), for brushing cakes
     Confectioners' sugar, for dusting

In a large bowl, sift together the dry ingredients. Stir in the warm milk and melted butter. Add the dissolved yeast and eggs. Knead until fairly smooth. Add the dried fruits, almonds, and lemon rind to the dough and continue kneading on a floured board for about 10 minutes. If dough is sticky, knead in more flour.

Place dough in a buttered bowl, cover with plastic wrap, and let rise in a warm place until doubled in bulk, about 1 to 2 hours. Punch down and cut dough into two parts. Roll each part into a 12 x 8 inch rectangle. Brush with the melted butter, then fold one long

edge to the center. Fold the other long edge to the center, overlapping by 1 inch. Turn over, taper the ends, and place on a parchment-lined baking sheet. Cover with plastic wrap and let rise again in a warm place for 1 to 1½ hours.

Preheat the oven to 350° F. Bake the stollen for 35 to 40 minutes, or until golden brown. Cool on rack and dust with confectioners' sugar.

SOUR CREAM CAKE

MAKES ONE 5 × 9–INCH LOAF

   ½ cup (1 stick) unsalted butter
1½ cups sugar
   4 large eggs, separated
   1 cup sour cream
   2 teaspoons lime juice
   1 teaspoon grated lime zest
   ½ teaspoon almond extract
1¾ cups sifted cake flour
   ½ teaspoon baking powder
   ¼ teaspoon baking soda

Preheat the oven to 325° F. Butter and flour the loaf pan.

Cream the butter and sugar until light. Add the egg yolks, sour cream, lime juice and zest, and almond extract. Continue mixing until fluffy. Sift together the dry ingredients and stir into the sour cream mixture. Beat the egg whites to soft peaks and gently fold into the batter.

Fill the pan three-fourths full with batter and bake for 50 to 55 minutes, or until a cake tester comes out clean. Remove from pan and cool on a rack.

FRUITCAKE

MAKES ONE 8-INCH CAKE

- 1 cup (2 sticks) unsalted butter, at room temperature
- 1 cup sugar
- 6 large eggs
- 2 pounds finely chopped candied fruits (equal amounts of citron, lemon peel, orange peel, cherries, apricots)
- 1 pound coarsely chopped pecans
- ¼ cup unsulphured molasses
- 1¼ cups sifted all-purpose flour
- 1 tablespoon ground allspice

GLAZE

- 1 cup apricot jam
- ⅓ cup brandy

GARNISH

Whole dried apricots, Chinese apples, cherries, figs, and pecan halves

Preheat the oven to 275° F. Butter a 3-inch deep, 8-inch round cake pan. Line the bottom and sides with wax paper, butter again, and then dust with flour.

Cream the butter and sugar until light. Add the eggs one at a time, beating until fluffy. Stir in the fruits, nuts, and molasses. Sift the flour with the allspice and stir into the batter until well mixed.

Spoon the batter into the prepared cake pan. Set the pan in a roasting tin with 1½ to 2 inches of hot water. Bake for 3 to 3½ hours, or until cake tester comes out clean. Cool in pan on a cake rack.

Remove cake from pan and pull off the wax paper. Strain the apricot jam and heat with the brandy. Glaze the cake, decorate with garnishes, and glaze again. Wrap and store in a cool place.

Bearing gifts we traverse afar
Field and fountain,
Moor and mountain . . .
　　　　John Henry Hopkins, Jr.

After several years of giving homemade gifts like a jar of jam, or a bottle of scented vinegar, or a plum pudding, or shortbread, I began a tradition of gift baskets. First I made them for my friends and family, then for business associates and corporate clients, until we found ourselves filling hundreds of baskets, each unique. We have also filled pottery batter bowls, wallpaper- or fabric-covered hatboxes, copper trays, or Shaker boxes. The packing is very important: we use lots of colored tissue, ribbon, and cellophane. The contents may include tablecloths and napkins; woollen throws; wreaths; cakes, cookies, teas; antique cutlery; gardening tools, seeds, bulbs; smoked turkeys and quails; and relishes, chutneys, sauces, and jams. One way we make our baskets unique is to create each one around a theme: a basket for the birds, a pet's basket, tea for six, a gardener's basket, or whatever. If you think about the recipient and his or her favorite pleasures, a theme will always suggest itself.

Opposite: I often tuck potpourri into my gift baskets—sometimes in an antique lace-trimmed linen handkerchief so it can be used as a sachet.

Above: The best Christmas gifts are those I would love for myself—like these antique cookie cutters.

A GIFT FOR A NATURE LOVER

A great, flat handmade willow basket was covered with sheet moss, then filled with:

> *Birdhouses designed by Zacki*
> *Birdseed in cellophane bags*
> *A nut ball (shelled filberts, raisins, and rosehips rolled together with suet and tied with a golden ribbon*
> *A birdseed heart (a twig frame covered with almond butter, lard, and peanut butter, and rolled in thistle seed)*
> *A pinecone covered with nut butters and coated with birdseed*
> *A tiny gold-leafed pumpkin*
> *Two twig pot scourers*
> *A bunch of natural wheat, tied Scandinavian-style*

ZACKI'S SOUTHERN HERITAGE BASKET

> *Boiled peanuts*
> *Pecan-walnut praline*
> *Stuffed figs and dates*
> *Potted cheese*
> *Moravian molasses cookies*
> *New Year's hoppin' John*
> *Sour cream cake*
> *Purple basil jelly*
> *Lemon jelly*
> *Zacki's own potpourri*
> *Herb-log fire starters*
> *A Moravian cookie cutter*

The filled basket was wrapped in yards of clear cellophane, tied with a wide turquoise satin ribbon, and topped with a bittersweet berry wreath.

MARTHA'S FRIENDSHIP BASKET

A Christmas pudding
Tea-smoked chicken
Curried spiced nuts
Cayenne pepper wafers
Scotch shortbread scallops
Chamomile tea
Mulled wine mix
An old edition of Emerson's essays
on nature
Pretty floral napkins

A double-lidded ash picnic hamper (handmade for us by a wonderful family in Oregon) was lined with a large picnic cloth; I tucked in some homemade jellies, flavored vinegar, and mincemeat, and placed the basket under the tree to await Christmas Eve.

A GIFT OF FLOWERS

This is such an easy gift to assemble, and so well received:

A dozen narcissus bulbs
Crushed stone
Sheet moss
A waterproof saucer

Each item—everything needed to force a bowl of narcissi—is packed in cellophane and tied with a festive ribbon. Don't forget to include planting instructions!

WREATHS & TOPIARIES

Unbidden earth shall wreathing ivy bring
And fragrant herbs (the promises of Spring)
As her first offerings to her infant king.

Virgil

Growing up, we made our own wreaths for our house on Elm Place. I don't think we did anything too extravagant, but we always enjoyed the feeling of accomplishment. Nowadays, the art of making wreaths and topiaries has assumed a new dimension. Walking in the city last Christmas, I was struck by the beauty of the decorations: the sculptured boxwood garlands at Bergdorf's; the flower-studded topiaries in the windows at Ralph Lauren. These florists' creations are very, very costly, but with ingenuity, wreaths and topiaries just as lovely can be made at home.

This year we made wreaths for inside and out, and color coordinated them with the rooms and passageways in which they were displayed. We left behind the traditional red and green color scheme of Christmases past; instead we concentrated on golds, bright yellows, burnished oranges, aquas, and blues. When each creation took its place, we were thrilled to feel again the accomplishment of making something beautiful.

Opposite: My favorite wreath this year was made from noble fir and decorated with teal blue silk moiré ribbon bows and dried blue hydrangeas.

Above: The gilded Federal mirror, above the dining room mantel heaped with evergreens and silvered glass balls, reflects soft candlelight.

BLUE HYDRANGEA WREATH

1. Each summer and fall, I dry many flowers from my garden—hydrangeas are among the most rewarding. Unlike most blossoms, which must be dried in silica gel for the best results, hydrangeas can just be hung upside down in a dark room; they will retain their color and form beautifully.

2. Simple evergreen wreaths can be made at home, or bought from florists and Christmas tree farms. We found a man in New York this year who created many wreaths of different sizes, including this 30-inch circle of noble fir, a bluish short-needled conifer. It was the perfect background for the hydrangea blooms, whose stems were long and stiff enough to hold them in place without wire or glue.

3. The ribbon was tied into bows of equal sizes, which were then attached to the evergreen with florist's wire.

4. I attached this wreath to the wall in my parlor with picture wire wrapped securely around a small screw, which is painted to match the wall and can thus remain from one Christmas to the next.

Opposite: While I was making the wreath, some of the blue blossoms fell from the hydrangea clusters. The color was so beautiful that I filled bowls with the flowers and put them on tables in the parlor; I put a clove pomander in each bowl so that the flowers appeared to have a wonderful scent of their own.

LONG-LIVED EVERGREEN WREATH

1. I soaked a quantity of sheet moss in water until it was green and plump, and then surrounded a purchased wire wreath mold with the moss, wrapping it around the frame, until I had a good, fat wreath.

2. I cut a plastic trash bag into 4-inch-wide strips and wrapped them tightly around the moss, securing the ends with florist's "U" pins or thin wire. (The plastic holds the moss and retains moisture that will keep the evergreen cuttings fresh.)

3. The cuttings were arranged around the wreath; I clustered each type of evergreen a bit to give each section of wreath a unique color and texture. I stripped about 2 inches from the bottom of each cutting, then poked the stems through the plastic and secured them with more floral pins.

4. With a hook made from heavy wire, I placed the wreath in a semishady location; this type of wreath looks especially good outdoors, but will last indoors for a bit more than a week in a cool spot.

NOTE: *For our wreath, we used boxwood, blue cedar, arborvitae, fir, leucothoe, spruce, southern white cedar, andromeda, red dogwood, holly, and sumac.*

Sheet moss can be found in floral supply centers. It comes dried and seems rather lifeless, but soaked in cool water, the moss turns green and becomes springy.

ROSEBUD WREATH

1. Using a hot-glue gun, I applied dampened sheet moss to a heart-shaped straw wreath form. I completely covered the straw, piecing the moss when necessary.

2. Dried roses and rosebuds were arranged in clusters around the heart. I put a little hot glue on the underside of each flower and pressed it onto the moss.

3. Around each cluster of roses, I glued dried bay leaves onto the heart. The roses were so plump and luscious that no other ornamentation was necessary—no ribbons or bows or sparkles.

4. The completed rosebud wreath could be hung on a door or wall, but I simply laid it on the table in the library.

NOTE: *Straw wreath forms in various shapes are available at floral supply stores.*

Dried roses are easily made at home; for perfect blossoms, the best method is drying in silica gel, a white granulated powder that looks very much like sugar.

Flower heads are carefully placed in a shallow layer of the gel and then completely covered. Within 5 to 10 days, each blossom has been perfectly preserved, and the color and texture of the flower are almost identical to those of the living bloom.

REINDEER MOSS WREATH · PINECONE WREATH

1. This icy-gray reindeer moss on the wreath at left is so light it can be fixed to any kind of form— straw, moss, or plastic foam— with a hot-glue gun.

2. The pinecones above, however, need a sturdy base; a wire or vine wreath would be best. Large cones can be attached to the form with floral wire; smaller cones are attached to the larger ones with hot glue. Our pinecones came from California, Tennessee, Connecticut, and Massachusetts. After gathering, they were washed in cool water, dried, and sorted. For a shinier wreath, spray them with a semigloss or glossy lacquer.

Following pages: Using bases of plastic foam, twig and vine forms, and even chicken wire, we made topiaries in many different sizes and shapes this Christmas. My favorites were the little "standard" topiaries we made to surround the gingerbread house. Oasis, which in green foamy blocks is often used to support flower arrangements, makes a very secure holder for standard topiaries during construction; stems can be fashioned from store-bought wooden dowels, or cuttings from rosebushes, trees, or shrubs. (I like to find young saplings that have been marked by vines.)

COCKSCOMB TOPIARY

1. A tall grapevine-and-wire cone-shaped form made a suitable base for this topiary. I dampened large pieces of sheet moss to make them malleable, then wrapped them around the form and secured them with milliner's wire (very light, coated wire on spools). The moss was allowed to dry in place.

2. Beginning at the top of the tree, and using a hot-glue gun, I covered the moss with flower heads from dried cockscombs in pink and deep burgundy tones.

3. Working between the cockscombs, I studded the tree with other decorations. Ours included deep mauve rosebuds, filberts, tiny pomegranates that had been dusted with clear glitter, and small silver balls.

BITTERSWEET HEART & WREATH

1. These bittersweet berries were so Christmasy and yet so simple, I couldn't resist using them to make a small wreath and a heart-shaped decoration. I cut berries in small clusters from the branches and glued them onto plastic-foam forms until no base could be seen.

2. With bright satin ribbons, they were attached to gift baskets and hung about the house.

Following pages: A dried fern basket covered inside and out with dampened sheet moss and decorated with dried rosebuds and bay leaves makes a delightful container for lady apples from our orchard; it could also hold sugared fruit, nuts, or gifts.

Among the other boughs gilded apples and walnuts were
suspended, looking as though they had grown there.
Hans Christian Andersen

When I decided to create this year's holiday decor without relying on the red and green theme that has dominated our Christmas aesthetic, I thought it would be interesting to try gilding a few decorations. Two weeks later, almost everything in the house—from pomegranates and pinecones and evergreen boughs to homemade wrapping paper—had been dipped and brushed in dense, rich metallic paints and my sister Laura had renamed this book *Martha's Gilt Trip.*

Old art books and antiques provided us with inspiration. The goldsmith Benvenuto Cellini would have loved the molten gold pomegranates and the rich golden bay leaf wreaths. The English woodcarver Grinling Gibbons might even have approved of the elaborate centerpiece of gilded

nuts, seed pods, dried woodland mushrooms, and bromeliads. It's true, we did get carried away, but the results were truly enchanting, and our house has never felt more full of light than it did this Christmas.

Opposite: Myriad gifts, wrapped in my own homemade gilt papers and tied with gold and copper ribbons, are piled on the library chair—with a tag-sale needlepoint pillow alongside.

Above: Teeny and Weeny curled up on a Lloyd Loom wicker chair.

GILDED WRAPPING PAPER

1. For all my Christmas gilding, I used an excellent metallic paint called Lust R Gild enamel made by W. H. Kemp, a division of Absolute Coatings Inc. of the Bronx, New York. Lust R Gild enamel comes in gold and copper shades, and results in a leaflike finish—far more subtle and beautiful than a metallic spray paint. For dipping or painting, I transfer the paints into larger plastic or foil containers.

While working with oil-based paints, I always cover my work table with several layers of newspaper, and I wear thin rubber surgical gloves. Because metallic paint is toxic—and has a very strong smell—I work in a well-ventilated room, or on the porch.

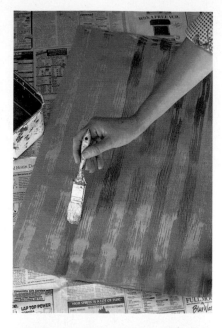

2. Using plain brown paper as the base, I applied the paint in different ways for different effects. The striped paper was made by dragging a 1-inch bristle brush dipped in gold in one direction, and another brush, dipped in copper, in the other direction.

3. This "spattered" paper was made by dripping and drizzling gold and copper paint from bristle brushes.

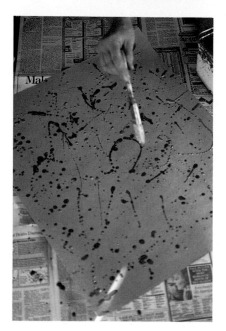

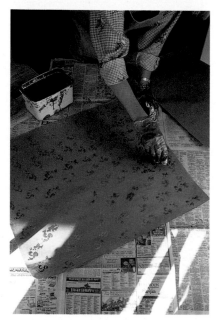

4. The "sponged" paper is very easy to make: I cut a natural rough-textured sponge into smallish pieces, dipped a piece just a bit into the paint, and pressed it lightly onto the paper in a random pattern.

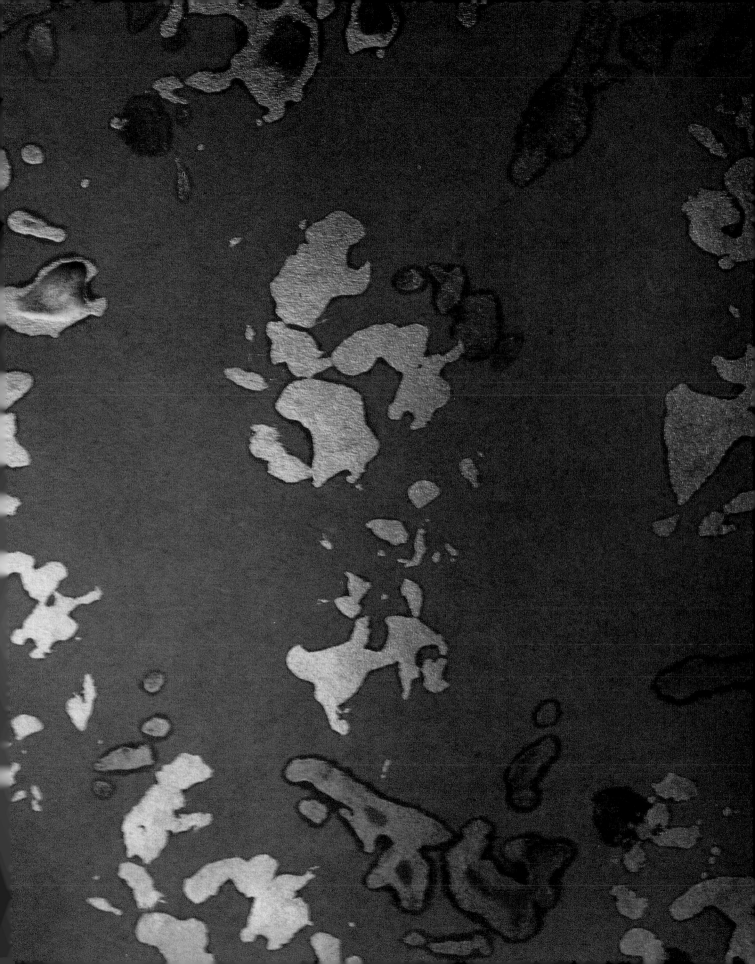

Right: Pinecones, nuts, cinnamon sticks, chestnuts, large and small pomegranates, bay leaves, and nutmegs are some of the objects we gilded with gold and copper paints. Once dipped, the pinecones drip dry over the paint can, or a tray set to catch excess paint.

Below: Just-dipped pomegranates and walnuts on an old cake rack; in 15 to 20 minutes they will be dry enough to handle.

Opposite: On the kitchen mantel, an antique black urn filled with gilded pinecones and pomegranates sits amid garlands of fresh, fragrant bay leaves and yards of gauzy golden ribbon.

GILDED CENTERPIECE

1. On a visit to England, I stayed in a house graced by woodcarvings by the 17th-century craftsman Grinling Gibbons. Returning home, I thought it would be fun to recreate a "Gibbons" as a centerpiece for my Christmas table —but while Gibbons's fruits and flowers were laboriously carved from wood, I used the real thing: seed pods, lotus pods, woodland mushrooms, miniature bromeliads, star anise, and ferns, all gathered on winter walks and then dipped in metallic paint.

2. By applying hot glue generously to the stems of the large objects, I was able to make them adhere securely to the gold-painted base of plastic foam.

3. The completed centerpiece was so beautiful I created a golden table around it for my Christmas Day dinner.

Opposite: By using objects from nature and a subtle metallic enamel, we made gilded decorations that were not at all gaudy or ostentatious.

Following pages: Dried bay leaves were gilded and then glued to a twig form to make this exquisite golden wreath.

CHRISTMAS TREES

The Yule trees, and the dreams all children dream
The tremulous glow of candles in rows,
The gold and silver of angels and globes
And the splendor of tinsel and toys under trees.

Boris Pasternak

In 1947, my father decided to cut down the tall but straggly blue spruce in our front yard. The first twenty feet of tree were sparse, and the boughs much too large for any room in our house, but the top ten feet made the fullest, roundest, and most perfect tree any of us had ever seen. We decorated it with large, pointed colored lights, my mother's collection of old ornaments, about a dozen boxes of real lead tinsel, and about fifty yards of colorful chains I made from construction paper, highlighted every few inches with a ring of precious silver or gold foil.

We still have fun with our trees: we had three this year (not counting the fruit trees outside, which were strung with twinkling white lights) and each was designed to draw people to it with a story of friends (Zacki's "tree for the birds"), children (the popcorn-ball tree in the barn), or family tradition (the library tree with its years of tag-sale ornaments).

Opposite: It is possible to find many very natural and realistic tree ornaments, like the sweet birds that decorated the balsam on our porch. They make a delightful change from glass and glitter.

Above: Our garden cart came in very handy when moving the large cut evergreen trees into place.

A TREE FOR THE BIRDS

1. We have collected many different types of little stuffed and carved bird ornaments over the years. They can be secured to branches with wire or raffia ties.

2. To create a setting for our birds' tree, we tacked and glued branches of fir trees to the window frames of the porch and decorated them with little birds and lights.

3. To decorate our floor-to-ceiling balsam, miniature white lights were first twined through the branches. Tiny birdhouses, designed by my friend Zacki, were tucked in, and golden gauze ribbon was used as garlanding. Then we made nests from Spanish moss and filled them with the birds and little colored wooden eggs. The tree was lovely by day and by night—an objective to keep in mind when decorating any tree.

Following pages: For the last 25 years or so, I've been collecting old glass balls and ornaments—every time I go to a tag sale, I check all the boxes of oddments. I give some away—they make charming Christmas gifts—and the rest go on the tree in the library, an eight-foot-tall Douglas fir this year. When I can find heavy lead tinsel like the kind we had as children, I hang it from the boughs, but even when it's not available, the old-fashioned ornaments make the tree sparkling and festive. The library needed little other decoration: celadon silk ribbons garlanded through the chandeliers, a silver compote of red roses to scent the room, and, of course, a heap of gilded presents under the tree.

CHILDREN'S TREE

1. We chose to decorate the tree with bows of dark green paper ribbon—an inexpensive but effective ornament. The ribbon comes in a snakelike coil and must be carefully unfurled.

2. Melissa tied the big bows, keeping them all approximately the same size, and gently fanning out the ribbon.

3. More than 50 bows were used on this huge tree; extras went in among the evergreen garlands.

Opposite: The decorations in the barn were simple and rustic—garlands of evergreens in the rafters, piles of pinecones on the mantel, and a noble fir wreath over the massive fireplace. The centerpiece was a full, sturdy blue spruce, thirteen feet tall.

POPCORN BALLS

4 tablespoons (¹/₂ stick) unsalted
    butter
1 10-ounce bag marshmallows
¹/₄ cup light brown sugar
3 quarts popped popcorn

In a large heavy pot, melt the
butter over low heat. Add the
marshmallows and brown sugar
and stir until melted. Remove
from heat.

Place the corn in a large bowl and
pour on the marshmallow mixture;
toss well. Butter your hands and
shape the corn into balls of
whatever size you desire. Set on
wax paper to dry.

*Right: About 10 days before
Christmas, some of my littlest friends
came by to help make the popcorn-ball
decorations for the barn tree. Left to
right, here are Olivia Zaleski,
Katharine Zaleski, Christen
Hartnett, and Peter Beer.*

*Above: My niece, Sophie Martha
Herbert, took her work very seriously.*

Above: We use the same little battery-powered white lights from year to year. Before twining them through our trees, we lay out the strings and test for burned-out bulbs, repairing and replacing when necessary.

Right: Marsha Harris and Jennifer Levin came to the holiday party bearing the gift of a live flower wreath from the florist Paul Bott. The front path to the house is lined with a double row of apple trees, and they are always decorated with many little lights at Christmastime.

THE GINGERBREAD MANSION

This is meeting time again. Home is the magnet. . . .
All that is dear, that is lasting, renews its hold on us:
we are home again. . . .

Elizabeth Bowen

Each year I vow never, never, never to make another gingerbread house. And each year something makes me break that vow, resulting in the best house ever. It was the same this year.

I don't know what induced me to build gingerbread houses in the first place, nor what inspired me to make them so large and elaborate. Over the years I have made country cottages, town houses—once even a huge Viennese baroque church for the family of Ronald Lauder, our ambassador to Austria. This year I wanted to make a house that was similar to my own Turkey Hill Federal farmhouse, but its proportions and window sizes got a bit exaggerated—and my real home, unlike its gingerbread replica, lacks a gold-leaf roof. But that's the beauty of a ginger-

bread house: frustrated architects, decorators, and contractors will delight in this lovely work, as will the children of the house, who take the whole thing so much in stride.

Opposite: The gingerbread mansion was glorious this year. A fanciful copy of my own house (I took lots of artistic license), it was placed on the small sideboard in the dining room.

Above: It snowed right at the best time, a few days before our Christmas party.

GINGERBREAD FOR GINGERBREAD MANSION

½ cup (1 stick) margarine, at room
  temperature
½ cup loosely packed dark brown
  sugar
½ cup unsulphured molasses
3½ cups sifted all-purpose flour
  1 teaspoon baking soda
  1 teaspoon ground cinnamon
  1 teaspoon ground ginger
½ teaspoon salt
¼ teaspoon cloves
⅓ cup water

Cream together the margarine and
sugar. Add the molasses and
continue mixing until well
incorporated.

Sift the dry ingredients together.
With the mixer on low speed, add
the dry ingredients alternating
with the water. If the dough
becomes too stiff, add the last bit
of flour by hand.

Work the dough with your hands
until it becomes smooth in
consistency. Turn out onto plastic
wrap, form into a neat rectangle,
wrap well, and chill thoroughly.

After all the pieces have been cut
out, bake at 350° F. for 10–15
minutes, or until firm but not
browned.

*I took architectural drawing in high
school, and I have never regretted the
hours spent with ruler and T square.*

THE GINGERBREAD MANSION

1. Designing a gingerbread house is just like drawing plans for a real structure: the first step is to figure out overall dimensions based on the size of your site—or, in the case of a gingerbread house, based on the size of your oven and your baking sheets.

2. I bake my house pieces on heavy black steel pans from France. First the pans are sprayed with vegetable oil, and then the dough is rolled directly onto the sheets using as little flour as possible. For the sides and roof, because they must be very strong, I roll out two pieces of dough on top of each other.

3. The house pattern is cut from parchment paper or brown construction paper. It is laid atop the rolled dough, and cut out with the point of a sharp knife. Excess dough is removed, and the pieces are chilled until ready to bake. Once baked, the gingerbread is cooled on racks and stored in a dry, cool place, lying absolutely flat. (I wrap the gingerbread pieces, baking sheets and all, in plastic wrap, and find they keep well for a week this way.)

4. The day before you erect the house, decorate the pieces with the royal icing, making the architectural details as fancy as you wish. The consistency of the icing must be perfect, neither too runny nor too stiff: 3 egg whites to 1½ pounds of sifted confectioners' sugar is about right. I make my decorations with a round #2 icing tip and a flexible nylon bag.

5. After the house pieces have been decorated, I make sugar windows by pouring melted, slightly caramelized sugar onto parchment paper. I try to make each window just slightly larger than the opening.

6. With the #2 icing tip, I pipe the sashes and bars onto the windows.

7. "Glue" icing is made by beating royal icing very stiffly in an electric mixer until fluffy and light. It has a lot of volume, and is used in large quantities to hold the house pieces together. Here I pipe it with a large tip on the wrong side of the house around the window openings; the windows are then pressed into the glue.

8. Allow the gingerbread to lie flat until the icing holding the windows is quite hard.

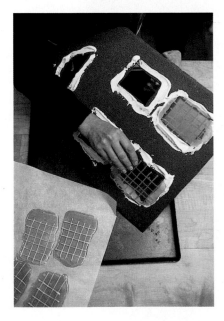

9. When erecting a large house like this one, I get help from a friend—a very patient friend. Working on the wrong side of the gingerbread piece, I pipe a fat strip of glue icing along one edge of the front and a side piece. With the two pieces held in place, I spread more icing with a spatula along the inside of the joint.

10. Two large pieces, the front and the back, standing with one side in place. I build the house on a board or tray on which it can remain all during the display; a footed piece of plywood or an extremely stiff baking sheet is perfect.

11. The exterior corners of the house may have oozing icing; it can be removed with a spatula, and a decorative edge piped on instead.

12. To make the four sides stay together without any chance of collapse, push several straight pins into each joint, through the front or back and into the sides. I leave the pins protruding just a tiny bit, and I can remove them right before I put the house on display.

13. This year, I gave the house a gold-leaf roof on one side, a copper roof on the other. The gold leaf is particularly thin, and must be handled very gently.

14. I picked up a sheet of leaf with a sable paintbrush, and very gently placed it on the roof, which had first been brushed with lightly beaten egg white.

15. The leaf was flattened onto the roof with another soft brush; I tried to cover the gingerbread completely, but found that any imperfections looked quite charming.

16. To create a shingled look, I piped royal icing in straight horizontal lines, then made little vertical lines at random; icing dots simulated nailheads.

Following pages: The facade of the gingerbread mansion, with its glistening windows and golden roof. Little white battery-operated lights brighten the interior (I left one window opening empty so the lights could be inserted after the house was completed). Topiary trees, juniper cuttings, and gilded pinecones create a landscape around the house.

We bring in the holly, the ivy, the pine,
The spruce and the hemlock together we twine;
With evergreen branches our walls we array
For the keeping of Christmas, our high holiday.

English carol

Yet another family tradition began when Andy and I celebrated our first Christmas on Riverside Drive. We had a spacious apartment with a wonderful flow from room to room, and we found that we could easily entertain eighty or ninety for cocktails. That first year, the invitation read "Christmas Carols, Cocktails, and Desserts," and this theme has persisted over the years with the addition of more hors d'oeuvres, and a hearty one-course supper for late departees.

This year more than 175 guests came for "Christmas All Over the House," to begin at 6 P.M. and end whenever. Hors d'oeuvres were served in the outside kitchen, a buffet supper was laid out in the barn, and champagne, eggnog, and desserts were in the main house. It was a clear night, there was a bit of a moon, and the sky was filled with stars. The paths were lined with hundreds of paper-bagged candles, and the fruit trees and windows shone with little white lights. It was festive, but simple, warm, and welcoming and friendly—all that a gathering of family and friends should be.

Opposite: On the night of the party, the house looked warm and bright.

Above: A luminaria—a brown paper bag filled with sand nestling a night light—glows on the path to the barn.

CASSOULET

SERVES 100

14 *quarts chicken stock*
16 *pounds Great Northern white beans, washed and drained*
6 *5-pound ducks*
3 *teaspoons salt*
2½ *teaspoons freshly ground black pepper*
10 *sprigs fresh thyme*
2 *10-pound geese*
20 *sage leaves*
3 *6-pound legs of lamb*
12 *pounds pork loin*
5 *pounds pancetta, cut into ½-inch cubes*
2 *cups fresh duck fat*
16 *cloves garlic, finely chopped*
10 *pounds yellow onions, finely chopped*
4 *32-ounce cans whole plum tomatoes, drained*
3 *bottles dry white wine*
  Large bunch parsley
10 *bay leaves*
8 *leeks, washed and chopped*
8 *carrots, peeled and cut into chunks*
10 *whole cloves*
6 *pounds garlic sausage*

Opposite above: Making cassoulet for 100 is a three-day process.

Opposite middle: Two huge casseroles of cassoulet with their bread crumb topping, ready to go into the oven for their final browning.

Opposite below: For such a big party —almost 200 guests—I need help from the family. My sister Laura prepared the baked smoked ham and the country ham, using a recipe that's really quite simple though it takes two days to complete.

TOPPING

6 *cups fresh white bread crumbs*
2 *cups finely chopped parsley*
10 *cloves garlic, very finely chopped*

Fill two very large pots with the chicken stock, add the beans, and boil for 20 minutes. Skim the surface of foam and allow beans to cool in the liquid.

Preheat the oven to 450° F. Season ducks with 2 teaspoons of salt, 2 teaspoons of pepper, and 3 sprigs of thyme. Roast on racks for 30 minutes. Season geese with remaining salt and pepper, and sage. Roast on racks for 1 hour.

Bone the lamb and pork. Roast the bones in the oven for 30 minutes. Cut lamb and pork meat into 2-inch cubes. Melt ½ cup of duck fat in a very large skillet, and brown the lamb cubes one layer at a time. Continue with pork, adding duck fat as necessary. Continue with pancetta. Set meat aside.

Add remaining fat to the skillet and sauté the garlic and onions until golden, 5 minutes. Add tomatoes, two bottles of wine, two sprigs of thyme, half the parsley, and 5 bay leaves. Simmer for 15 minutes, then add to the boiled beans.

Cut the breast meat from ducks and geese. Cut legs into two pieces; bone thighs. Cut off the wings and chop off the wing tips. Cut the breast and thigh meat into small pieces and set aside with drumsticks and wings.

Skim excess liquid off the top of the boiled beans and reserve. Wrap poultry carcasses, pork and lamb bones, leeks, carrots, cloves,

and the remaining herbs into two cheesecloth packets. Place amid beans, and simmer for 2 hours, or until beans are almost tender. Cool 1 hour, and refrigerate overnight, uncovered.

The following day, preheat the oven to 350° F. Bring bean mixture to a simmer, adding reserved bean liquid and the last bottle of wine. Poach the garlic sausage for 30 minutes, peel, and cut into ½-inch slices.

Remove the cheesecloth packets from the bean mixture. In two very large casseroles, layer the beans with the duck, goose, pancetta, pork, and lamb. Top with a layer of bread crumbs, parsley, and garlic. Bake for 2 to 3 hours, or until the topping has formed a light brown crust. Arrange garlic sausage on top, and serve hot.

BAKED SMOKED HAM

SERVES 20

1 *12 to 14 pound fully cooked smoked ham, bone in*
1 *cup packed dark brown sugar*
½ *cup Armagnac*

Preheat the oven to 325° F. and line a large baking pan with foil. Put the ham on the foil, fat side up. Wrap with another piece of foil and bake for about 2 hours.

With a sharp knife, trim excess fat from ham, leaving a layer about ⅛ inch thick. Score the fat in a small diamond pattern.

Mix together the brown sugar and the Armagnac to make a glaze. Lightly coat the ham with half of the glaze and return it to the oven, uncovered. After 10 minutes, coat again with the remaining glaze. Continue baking for another 20 minutes, then serve hot.

COUNTRY HAM

SERVES 20

1 *16-pound country-cured ham*
1 *cup packed dark brown sugar*
½ *cup red wine or port*

Soak ham in cold water for 12 hours.

Preheat the oven to 500° F. Line a large roasting pan with aluminum foil. Drain the ham and scrub it clean. Place the ham in pan; wrap well with another piece of foil. Bake for 30 minutes, then turn the oven off and allow the ham to sit in the closed oven (don't open it even once) for 3 hours.

With the ham still inside, turn the oven back on to 500° F. Wait 20 minutes, turn the oven off, and let the ham sit, again in the closed oven, for 12 hours. Remove ham from oven and unwrap.

Preheat the oven to 350° F. With a sharp knife, trim the rind and all but ¼ inch of the fat from the ham, then score the fat in a small diamond pattern.

Mix the brown sugar and wine or port to make a glaze. Lightly coat the ham with half the glaze and bake uncovered for 15 minutes. Coat again with the remaining glaze and bake for another 20 minutes. Serve the ham hot or cold.

PARTY SALAD

Allow 1 large handful of salad per person, a combination of watercress, arugula, radicchio, red leaf lettuce, and green leaf lettuce. Gently wash and dry the lettuces. Place in a serving bowl. Just before serving, whisk the vinaigrette and pour over the salad. Gently toss and serve.

VINAIGRETTE

- *⅔ cup olive oil*
- *⅓ cup balsamic vinegar*
- *3 tablespoons Dijon mustard*
- *1 tablespoon finely chopped shallot*
  Salt and freshly ground black pepper to taste

SOFT DINNER ROLLS

MAKES 2 DOZEN

- *1 package active dry yeast*
- *¼ cup warm water*
- *1 teaspoon sugar*
- *2 tablespoons (¼ stick) unsalted butter*
- *2 tablespoons solid vegetable shortening*
- *1 teaspoon salt*
- *2 cups milk*
- *4 cups sifted all-purpose flour*

Proof the yeast in the warm water with the sugar. Place the butter, shortening, and salt in a large bowl. Scald the milk and add to bowl. Stir until butter and shortening melt. Allow to cool slightly; add flour and stir. Add proofed yeast, mix thoroughly, and knead for 5 minutes. Cover bowl with plastic wrap and put in a warm place until dough has doubled in bulk, about 45 minutes.

Punch dough down and turn out onto a floured board. Roll dough ½ inch thick. Cut into 1-inch rounds. Place in parchment-lined pan, each roll touching the next, and put in a warm place until dough has redoubled in bulk, about 30 minutes. Preheat the oven to 375° F. Bake for 15 to 20 minutes and serve hot.

BUTTERMILK BISCUITS

MAKES 5 DOZEN

- *6 cups sifted all-purpose flour*
- *2 teaspoons salt*
- *1 teaspoon baking soda*
- *8 teaspoons baking powder*
- *1⅓ cups solid vegetable shortening*
- *2¼ cups buttermilk*

Preheat the oven to 450° F.

Sift flour, salt, baking soda, and baking powder into a large bowl. Place half the dry ingredients in a food processor, add the shortening, and process for 10 seconds, or just until the mixture resembles coarse meal. Return the flour and shortening mixture to the bowl containing the remaining dry ingredients. Using your fingers, continue to combine the dry ingredients and shortening. Add the buttermilk all at once and stir until the dough begins to stiffen, approximately 3 minutes.

Turn out the dough onto a well-floured board, dust lightly with flour and knead for a minute (no longer). Roll the dough ¼ inch thick, cut into 1½-inch rounds, pierce each biscuit with a fork, and place on a heavy cookie sheet. Bake for 12 minutes and serve hot.

BAGUETTE SANDWICHES

With a very thin, crusty French baguette as the base, these three different fillings can be used to make delicious sandwiches.

1. *Mayonnaise*
   Thinly sliced Japanese eggplant, brushed with olive oil and minced garlic, then broiled until lightly browned
   Crumbled goat cheese
   Fresh basil and flat leaf parsley
   Thinly sliced tomatoes
   Coarse salt and freshly ground black pepper

2. *Softened butter and cream cheese*
   Thinly sliced Italian salami
   Tender watercress
   Coarse salt and freshly ground black pepper

3. *Mayonnaise*
   Sliced plum tomatoes
   Olivata (calamata olive spread)
   Fresh basil leaves
   Coarse salt and freshly ground black pepper

Using a bread knife, slice the baguette, lengthwise, being careful not to slice all the way through. Layer the fillings generously from one end to the other, pushing down so the sandwich is stuffed fully.

Prior to serving, slice each baguette sandwich crosswise into 2-inch pieces.

Opposite: The buffet dinner was served from the long country table in the barn, where Winston's waiters kept things running smoothly.

CAYENNE PEPPER WAFERS

MAKES 6 DOZEN

- ½ pound Gruyère cheese, grated
- 1 cup (2 sticks) unsalted butter, at room temperature
- 1 teaspoon cayenne pepper
- 1 teaspoon salt
- 2½ cups sifted all-purpose flour
- 1 cup chopped walnuts or pecans

Cream the cheese and butter. Sift together the cayenne pepper, salt, and flour and add, gradually, to butter mixture. Add the nuts, mixing well. Divide the dough in half and shape into logs to 1½ inches in diameter. Wrap well and refrigerate for at least 1 hour.

Preheat the oven to 350° F. and line baking sheets with parchment paper.

With a sharp knife, cut the logs into ¼-inch slices; place the wafers 1 to 2 inches apart on baking sheets.

Bake for 15 to 20 minutes, until lightly colored. Cool on racks, then store in an airtight container.

Top: A choral group from Greens Farms Academy, my daughter's preparatory school in Westport, sang traditional carols for almost an hour.

Above: On the porch, guests were served champagne, white wine, or eggnog.

Opposite: Guests sat themselves down wherever they could to eat the buffet supper in the barn.

CROQUEMBOUCHE

PÂTE À CHOUX PUFFS

1½ sticks unsalted butter
1½ cups water
¼ teaspoon salt
1 teaspoon sugar
1½ cups sifted all-purpose flour
6 large eggs

GLAZE

1 egg beaten with 1 teaspoon water

MOCHA CRÈME PATISSIÈRE

6 egg yolks
½ cup sugar
½ cup sifted all-purpose flour
2 cups milk
3 tablespoons unsalted butter
2 ounces semisweet chocolate
2 teaspoons instant espresso with 2 teaspoons hot water

CARAMEL

2 cups sugar
⅔ cup water
2 tablespoons corn syrup

Preheat the oven to 425° F.

To make the puffs, melt the butter in the water with salt and sugar. Remove from heat, add the flour, return to heat and beat vigorously for 2 to 3 minutes. (A film should form on the bottom of the pan.) Cool slightly, and add eggs, one at a time, beating vigorously.

Using a pastry tube with a ½-inch opening, form 1-inch-high mounds, ¾ inch in diameter, on parchment-lined baking sheet. Glaze and smooth the tops. Bake for 20–25 minutes, until puffed and golden. Cool on racks.

To make the mocha cream, beat the egg yolks, gradually adding the sugar, until mixture is thick and pale yellow. Beat in the flour. Scald the milk and add in dribbles, reserving ½ cup for thinning. Return to clean pot and stir vigorously over high heat until mixture boils and thickens. If it seems too thick to pipe, add reserved milk. Remove from heat.

Add the butter, 1 tablespoon at a time. Melt the chocolate and add to mixture with the espresso. Just before assembling croquembouche, inject the cream into the puffs with a ¼-inch pastry tip.

To make the caramel, bring sugar, water, and corn syrup to a boil over high heat. Do not stir. Cover pan until steam dissolves any crystals. Uncover and boil 5 minutes, or until syrup is amber. Remove from heat. Dip the bottoms of the puffs, one by one, into the caramel and arrange in a pyramid. Cut the tip from a balloon whisk, dip into caramel, and whirl strands of caramel around croquembouche to form a spun-sugar web.

FRUIT TARTLETS

MAKES 30 TO 40 TARTLETS

2½ cups sifted all-purpose flour
1 teaspoon salt
1 teaspoon sugar (optional)
1 cup (2 sticks) unsalted butter, chilled and cut into small pieces
¼–½ cup ice water
1 cup Lemon Curd
1 cup Black Currant Curd
2 pints fresh raspberries, blackberries, currants, or a mixture

Put the flour, salt, and sugar in a food processor. Add the butter and process for 10 seconds. With the machine running, add ice water, drop by drop, until the dough holds together without being sticky. Do not process more than 30 seconds. Wrap dough and chill for at least 1 hour.

Assemble 2 1½–2½-inch tartlet pans for each shell you plan to bake. Spray the insides of half the tartlet pans with vegetable spray.

On a well-floured board, roll out the pastry until ⅛ inch thick. Press the pastry into the coated pans and remove excess with your thumb. Press a second, uncoated pan into each shell to act as a weight while baking. Place all the pans on a baking sheet and chill for at least 30 minutes.

Preheat the oven to 375° F.

Set another baking sheet on top of the tartlets to act as a weight and bake for 10 minutes, or until pastry edges begin to color. Remove the top baking sheet and the liner pans and continue to bake until the shells are golden, about 5 to 7 more minutes. Cool shells on racks.

Fill the shells with the fruit curds and garnish with berries.

Opposite: The crowning glory of the dessert table was, as usual, the croquembouche. Necy put this confection together while guests were being served hors d'oeuvres; she had to stand on a stool to spin the sugar around the tall mound of cream puffs.

A FESTIVE BREAKFAST

As I sat on a sunny bank,
On Christmas Day in the morning,
I spied three ships come sailing by.
English carol

Alexis is always home for Christmas Eve and Day, usually with a friend, and I ask other members of the family to join us for breakfast. If it's sunny, as it was this year, we set the breakfast table on the porch; if the day is cold and snowy, we eat in the kitchen next to the fire. There are eggs of some sort—our chickens' Christmas gift to us— freshly squeezed juices, and homemade muffins. While most of our holiday feasts are set by tradition by now, breakfast is one where we like to experiment: this year, inspired by interest in regional and ethnic cooking, we adopted a Southwestern theme.

Following Nutley tradition, we open our gifts on Christmas morning (though we sometimes have a preview, opening one or two gifts on Christmas Eve). After Alexis has roused us early and we're finished with our gift giving, we're all really ready for a hearty breakfast.

Opposite: Christmas Day breakfast was so delightful on the sun-filled porch. The glass table was set with colorful Luna García pottery, old silver, and cacti.

Above: A huge Brahma hen, with feathered feet, sits atop a stone pedestal in the chicken yard.

Top: I squeezed the pomegranates on a Hamilton Beach juicer.

Middle: Each guest was served a small bowl of cheese grits, hot from the oven.

Above: The quince branch was surrounded by blue Aranucana eggs.

Opposite: The quince branch was decorated with Zacki's clay ornaments.

BREAKFAST BURRITOS

MAKES 4

  4 *flour tortillas*
  4 *large eggs*
  2 *tablespoons olive oil*
  2 *cups Breakfast Salsa (below)*
  1 *cup sour cream*
     Rosemary sprigs, for garnish
     Salt and freshly ground black
     pepper

Fill a medium saucepan with approximately 2 inches of water. Place a bamboo steamer or metal vegetable steamer in the pot and bring the water to a low boil over medium to low heat.

Wrap the tortillas in a towel and place in the steamer. Cover and steam for 5 minutes. Remove pot from the heat and set aside, covered, until ready to use the tortillas.

Fry eggs sunny-side up in hot olive oil. Place 1 tortilla on each plate, put 1 egg on top of each tortilla, and spoon ½ cup of salsa around each egg. Garnish the plates with sour cream and rosemary sprigs. Season with salt and pepper to taste.

BAKED CHEESE GRITS

SERVES 4 TO 6 GENEROUSLY

    4 *cups milk*
    2 *cups water*
1½ *cups quick-cooking grits*
 10 *tablespoons (1¼ sticks) unsalted butter*
    1 *teaspoon salt*
  ½ *teaspoon cayenne pepper*
    1 *cup grated cheddar cheese*
    3 *large eggs, lightly beaten*

Preheat the oven to 350° F. and butter a 2-quart baking dish.

In a large heavy saucepan, bring milk and water to a boil. Add the grits and, stirring from time to time, simmer until grits are done, 2 to 5 minutes.

Remove pan from heat and add the remaining ingredients. Pour into the buttered dish and bake for 30 to 40 minutes, until top is lightly browned. Serve hot.

BREAKFAST SALSA

MAKES 2 CUPS

 ½ *cup chopped scallions*
 ¼ *cup finely chopped cilantro*
  3 *ripe tomatoes, diced*
 ¼ *cup fresh-squeezed lemon juice*
  1 *red bell pepper, minced*
  1 *tablespoon rice vinegar*
 ½ *tablespoon peanut oil*
 ¼ *teaspoon Tabasco*
    Salt and freshly ground black pepper

Combine all ingredients in a bowl. Season to taste with salt and pepper.

TEQUILA BREAKFAST COCKTAIL

SERVES 4

  4 *cups fresh-squeezed orange juice*
 ½ *cup fresh-squeezed pomegranate juice*
 ½ *cup tequila*
  4 *tablespoons fresh lime juice*
    Lime wedges for garnish

Combine the liquids, pour into glasses, and garnish with lime wedges.

CHRISTMAS DAY DINNER

I love having a small, intimate dinner either on Christmas Eve or Christmas night. This year we were seven at the table, closest family and dearest friends. The house looked splendid: most of the party decorations were still fresh and festive. Two weeks before Christmas, I had been scouring tag sales for more decorations, and found by chance some lovely brown and copper luster plates decorated with winter reindeer scenes that simply made the dinner table glow.

The menu was an easy one; most of it could be prepared earlier in the day and reheated just before serving. The ducks were superb, especially crispy and savory—my guests agreed they were a lovely alternative to turkey and goose. Alexis, my vegetarian daughter, enjoyed the many other good things on the menu, and we ended the meal with a flaming Christmas pudding—one of the hundreds I had made back at the beginning of the season, and the beginning of this book.

Opposite: Christmas Day dinner for seven was served in my old kitchen. The table was set with ecru lace, Wedgwood plates in the Fallow Deer pattern, and Etruria plates with a copper-gold luster.

Above: A detail from my 18th-century copy of Correggio's Jupiter and Io.

133

ROASTED DUCKLINGS

SERVES 8 TO 10

3	6-pound ducks
2	tablespoons finely chopped garlic
1	tablespoon grated fresh ginger
2	tablespoons sesame oil
2	tablespoons honey
1/2	cup soy sauce
1/2	cup dry white wine
1/4	cup hoisin sauce
1	large tart apple, cut into thirds
1	orange, cut into thirds
3	celery stalks
18	sprigs fresh parsley
12	sprigs fresh thyme
	Salt and ground black pepper

Rinse ducks under cool water, pat dry with a cloth, and place in a large steel or glass bowl. Combine garlic, ginger, oil, honey, wine, and sauces, pour over ducks, and refrigerate for a day, turning the ducks several times.

Preheat the oven to 400° F.

Stuff the cavity of each duck with 1 piece apple, 1 piece orange, a celery stalk, and 6 parsley sprigs. Sprinkle with salt and pepper.

With your fingers, carefully loosen the skin from the breasts of the ducks. Place 4 thyme sprigs under the skin of each breast. Truss the

Top: On the granite hearthstone, in front of the red embers, a simple, homey Christmas dinner is displayed.

Above: The Christmas pudding, Moravian molasses cookies, and gilded chocolate truffles.

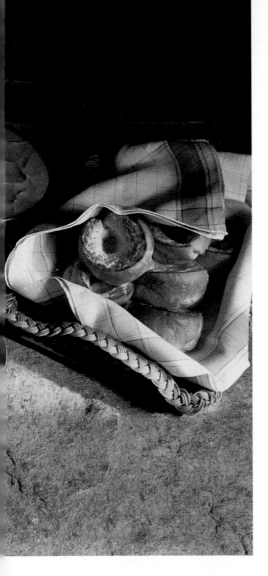

bird with butcher's twine. With a sharp fork, prick the skin on the back of each duck to help fat to flow out while roasting.

Line a large roasting pan with foil. Place the ducks breast side up on a rack in the roasting pan. Roast ducks approximately 1½ hours, or until internal temperature reaches 180° F., basting several times with boiling water. (This helps to dissolve the fat under the skin.) Remove ducks from oven, remove trussing string, and serve on a bed of Wild Rice, Chestnut, and Cranberry Dressing (recipe follows).

WILD RICE, CHESTNUT, AND CRANBERRY DRESSING

MAKES 8 CUPS

1½ *pounds fresh whole chestnuts*
 ½ *cup (1 stick) unsalted butter*
  3 *duck livers*
  6 *shallots, finely minced*
  4 *celery stalks, finely diced*
  2 *garlic cloves, finely minced*
  2 *cups wild rice*
  4 *cups chicken stock*
  1 *cup fresh cranberries*
 ½ *cup chopped Italian parsley*

Using a bottle opener, pierce the top and bottom of each chestnut. Put the chestnuts in a pot, cover with water, and bring to a boil. Lower heat and simmer for 10 minutes. Allow to cool slightly, then peel away the outer shells and skins while still warm. Set aside.

Melt 4 tablespoons of the butter in a skillet and sauté the duck livers for 10 minutes. Remove the livers and set aside. Melt the remaining butter and sauté the shallots, celery, and garlic for 3 to 4 minutes. Add the wild rice and stock to the skillet and bring to a boil. Reduce heat, cover, and simmer until rice is tender but not soft, approximately 45 to 50 minutes. Add more stock if necessary.

Finely mince the sautéed duck livers and add to the rice along with the fresh cranberries, parsley, and peeled chestnuts. Toss and place on a serving platter with roast ducks.

SAUERKRAUT AND FRESH CABBAGE WITH BROWNED MUSHROOMS

SERVES 8

  2 *pounds sauerkraut*
  8 *tablespoons (1 stick) unsalted butter*
  1 *pound fresh button mushrooms*
  6 *slices bacon, cut into 1-inch pieces*
  2 *onions, finely chopped*
  2 *garlic cloves, finely minced*
  2 *large tart apples, peeled, cored, and cut into wedges*
  2 *teaspoons caraway seeds*
  1 *small head green cabbage, cored and chiffonaded*
     Salt and freshly ground black pepper

In a colander, rinse the sauerkraut under cold water. Drain.

In a large skillet, melt 6 tablespoons of butter and sauté the mushrooms over low heat for 20 to 30 minutes, or until they become deep brown. Remove the mushrooms from the skillet and set aside. In the same skillet, fry the bacon until crisp. Remove from the pan and drain on paper towels. Sauté the onions and garlic in the bacon fat for 2 to 3 minutes. Add the drained sauerkraut, apple wedges, and caraway seeds. Cook slowly for about 15 minutes, stirring occasionally.

Meanwhile, in another skillet, melt the remaining butter and sauté the fresh cabbage for a few minutes, tossing until just tender.

Just before serving, combine the fresh cabbage with the sauerkraut, mushrooms, and bacon. Season to taste with salt and pepper. Reheat gently if necessary.

BROILED VEGETABLES

SERVES 8 TO 10

8 medium leeks
8 baby pattypan squash
½ cup (1 stick) unsalted butter
2 tablespoons olive oil
1 tablespoon finely minced fresh
    parsley or chervil
1 tablespoon finely minced fresh sage
4 small zucchini, cut lengthwise
    into strips
4 small yellow squash, cut into
    diagonal slices
2 yellow bell peppers, seeded and cut
    into quarters
2 red bell peppers, seeded and cut
    into quarters
2 Italian frying peppers, cut into
    quarters
    Salt and freshly ground black
    pepper

Peel outer leaves from leeks and
rinse bulbs under cold water.
Blanch leeks in boiling water for
10 minutes; remove and drain.
Rinse pattypan squash under cold
water and blanch in boiling water
for 5 minutes. Drain.

Melt the butter in a small
saucepan. Add olive oil and
minced herbs and set aside.
Preheat the broiler and line baking
sheets with foil.

*Opposite: Our Christmas dinner menu
could also work beautifully in a less
formal setting. On a long table in the
barn, I set Tepco portion plates in a
pinecone pattern with green-and-
yellow–handled Bakelite flatware on a
hand-stenciled canvas table covering.
A pinecone centerpiece and wreaths, old
green demilune shutters, potted juniper
and Wateriana miniatures, and
amethyst glass turkeys complete the
decorations.*

Arrange the vegetables on baking
sheets and brush with the butter
and oil mixture. Broil for 2 to 3
minutes, then turn vegetables
over, brush with more butter and
oil, and return to broiler for
another 2 to 3 minutes, until just
lightly browned. Arrange
vegetables on a platter, season
with salt and pepper, and serve.

BUTTERNUT SQUASH PUREE

SERVES 8 TO 10

4 tablespoons (½ stick) unsalted
    butter
1 onion, peeled and thinly sliced
1 butternut squash, peeled and cut
    into chunks
1 white turnip, peeled and sliced
2 ripe pears, peeled and cored
    Salt and pepper

Melt the butter in a large heavy
pot and sauté the onion until soft.
Add the squash, turnip, and pears
and simmer, covered, until soft,
about 15 minutes. If vegetables
become too dry, add a little water
to the pot.

Puree mixture in a food processor
until smooth. Season to taste with
salt and pepper.

CHRISTMAS SALAD

Allow 1 large handful of salad per
person, a combination of mâche
and radicchio. Gently wash and
dry the lettuces. Place in a serving
bowl. Immediately before serving,
whisk the vinaigrette and pour
over the salad. Gently toss and
serve.

LEMON CORIANDER VINAIGRETTE

1 tablespoon Champagne vinegar
1 tablespoon rice wine vinegar
½ teaspoon chopped fresh coriander
1 teaspoon lemon zest
6 tablespoons olive oil
    Salt and freshly ground black
    pepper to taste

HERB POPOVERS

MAKES 8

2 cups sifted all-purpose flour
¼ teaspoon salt
2 large eggs
1¾ cups milk
1 tablespoon butter, melted
¼ cup finely chopped fresh dill
¼ cup finely chopped fresh parsley

Preheat the oven to 450° F. and
oil 8 Pyrex 8-ounce custard cups.

Mix the flour and salt in a bowl.
In a separate bowl, beat the eggs
until frothy, add the milk and
melted butter, and continue to
beat vigorously.

Slowly add the egg and milk
mixture and chopped herbs to the
dry ingredients, stirring gently
until well blended. Be careful not
to overmix. Pour batter into
custard cups, half-filling them,
and place on a baking sheet.

Bake the popovers at 450° F. for
20 minutes, then reduce heat to
325° F. and continue baking for
another 15 minutes. Serve
immediately.

TRUFFLES OF GOLD

MAKES 4 DOZEN

    3 pounds semisweet chocolate,
       coarsely chopped
 1 1/2 cups crème fraîche
    5 tablespoons unsalted butter
    3 tablespoons cognac
  1/2 tablespoon solid vegetable
       shortening
   14 3-inch-square sheets of 23 karat
       gold leaf, torn carefully into
       quarters

Grind 1½ pounds of chocolate finely in a food processor. In a small heavy saucepan, bring the crème fraîche to a boil. With the processor running, pour the crème fraîche into the chocolate through the feed tube. Continue mixing until the chocolate is smooth, stopping as necessary to scrape down the sides of the work bowl. Refrigerate mixture in the covered processor bowl until cool, about 10 minutes.

Return the work bowl to the processor. Blend in the butter and cognac, scraping down sides of bowl. Transfer to another bowl, cover, and refrigerate for several hours, until firm enough to shape.

Using a miniature ice-cream scoop, form the chocolate into balls. Place on a parchment-lined baking sheet and refrigerate for approximately 10 minutes, until firm.

Place the remaining chocolate and the vegetable shortening in a metal bowl and melt in a 250° F. oven.

Roll each ball of chocolate with the palms of your hands until it is smooth. Using a wooden skewer,

pierce each truffle and dip into the melted coating chocolate. Gently place the dipped truffle on a clean piece of parchment. To decorate, gently press 1 quarter-sheet of gold leaf onto each truffle. Allow the coating chocolate to harden. Truffles can be kept, refrigerated, for up to 12 hours before serving.

BATTENBERG LACE

    3 cups sugar
    1 cup water
    3 tablespoons light corn syrup

Place all ingredients into a heavy pot, preferably a copper sugar pot. Cover with a lid and bring to a boil. Swirl (never stir) the pot until sugar dissolves, then uncover the pot and bring to a hard-crack stage, 300° F. on a candy thermometer. Syrup will be a light amber color; do not allow it to darken too much.

Remove pot from heat and immediately place in a bowl of cold water until syrup thickens a little. Drizzle the syrup from the pot onto parchment paper in a fine stream, making a decorative lace pattern. Allow to harden, then lift carefully off the parchment.

Top: I use a miniature ice-cream scoop to form the truffles.

Middle: With a bamboo skewer, I dip each truffle in melted chocolate.

Above: With sugar syrup, create a "doily" resembling Battenberg lace.

Opposite: When the chocolate coating has set, a small piece of 23K gold leaf is placed on top of each truffle.

HOLIDAY EGGNOG

SERVES 50

24 eggs, separated
2 cups granulated sugar
2 quarts whole milk
2 cups Bourbon
1 cup cognac
2 quarts heavy cream
Freshly grated nutmeg

Beat the egg yolks together with the sugar until the mixture is thick and creamy. Add the whole milk, the Bourbon, and the cognac. Stir well. (This mixture is the eggnog base and can be made a day or two in advance.)

Just before serving, whip the cream until soft peaks form. Whip the egg whites to a similar consistency and fold both the cream and the egg whites into the egg yolk mixture. Pour the eggnog into a very large bowl, sprinkle a grating of fresh nutmeg on top, and serve.

After dinner, friends and neighbors drop by for eggnog, served in front of the library tree from this immense Staffordshire punch bowl which I found at a local estate sale. It is decorated in teal blue on a pale green ground, and marked "ancient ruins" on the bottom. Over the years, I have collected many dozen glass punch cups in various patterns, and I use them for eggnog, mulled wine, and cider.

In the library, beneath a collection of Copeland's china by Spode, my daughter, Alexis, and her boyfriend, Sam Waksal, embrace in what they thought was a private moment.

INDEX

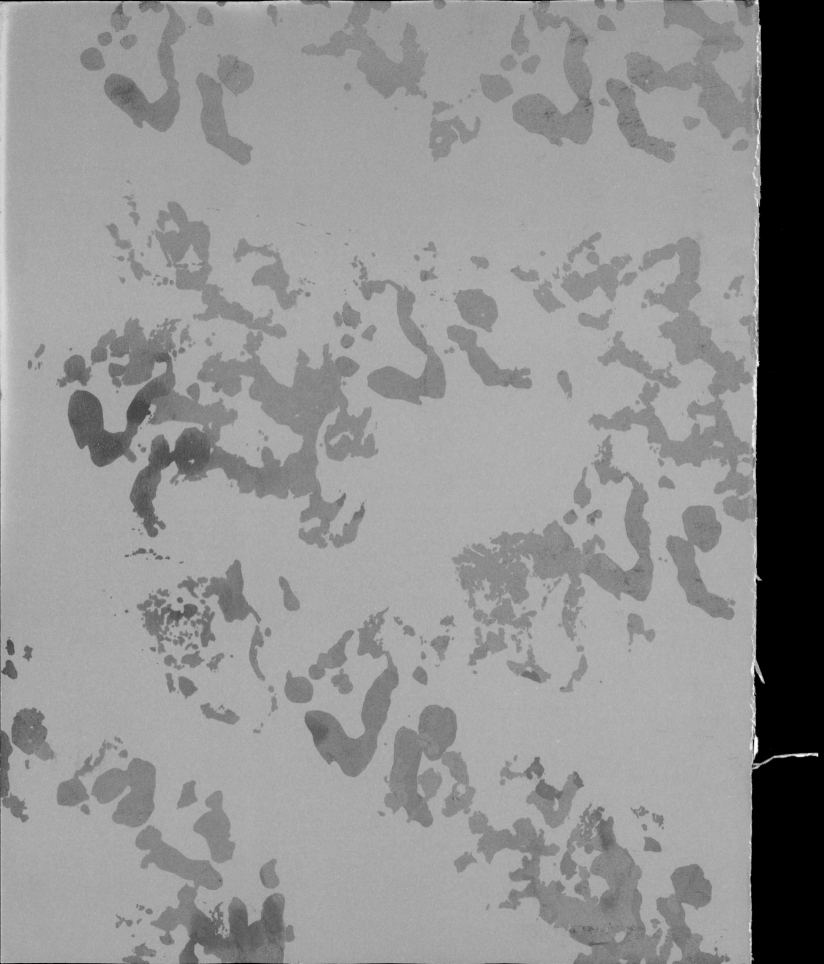